D0393948

CHRISTMAS
Memories

COMPILED BY

TERRY MEEUWSEN

A
JANET
THOMA
BOOK

THOMAS NELSON PUBLISHERS
Nashville • Atlanta • London • Vancouver

Published in Nashville, Tennessee, by Thomas Nelson, Inc.,
Publishers, and distributed in Canada by Word Communications,
Ltd., Richmond, British Columbia.

Unless otherwise noted, Scripture quotations are from THE NEW
KING JAMES VERSION. Copyright © 1979, 1980, 1982,
Thomas Nelson, Inc., Publishers.

Scripture quotations noted KJV are from The King James
Version of the Holy Bible.

Scripture quotations marked NIV are taken from the HOLY
BIBLE, NEW INTERNATIONAL VERSION ® . Copyright
© 1973, 1978, 1984 by International Bible Society. Used by
permission of Zondervan Publishing House. All rights reserved.

"Marty's Secret" by Diane Rayner reprinted with permission
from *Guideposts* magazine. Copyright © 1993 by Guideposts,
Carmel, NY 10512.

1-12-05   *12.99*

"A Song for Elizabeth" by Robin Cole reprinted with permission
from *Guideposts* magazine. Copyright © 1979 by Guideposts,
Carmel, NY 10512.

"I Knew You Would Come" by Elizabeth King English reprinted
with permission from *Guideposts* magazine. Copyright © 1983
by Guideposts, Carmel, NY 10512.

"The Kidnapped Doll" by Myrtle "Cookie" Potter reprinted
with permission from *Guideposts* magazine. Copyright © 1994
by Guideposts, Carmel, NY 10512.

Library of Congress Cataloging-in-Publication Data

Christmas memories / [compiled by] Terry Meeuwsen.
    p. cm.
    Cover title: Christmas memories from our hearts to yours.
    ISBN 0-7852-7253-4
    1. Christmas. 2. Christian biography—United States. 3. Women—United
States—Biography. I. Meeuwsen, Terry Anne. II. Title: Christmas memories
from our hearts to yours
BV45.C576   1996
263'.91—dc20   96-31229
                                           CIP

Printed in the United States of America.
1 2 3 4 5 6 — 01 00 99 98 97 96

Dedication

To Mom and Dad with a heart full of
thanks for a *lifetime* of memories.

CONTENTS

CONTENTS

Part Three
Creating the Memories of Christmas Future:
Ideas for Christmases to Come

CONTENTS

Part Four
A Diary of Christmas Memories:
From Your Heart to Those You Love

Acknowledgments

This book is not just a collection of individual stories and traditions, it is a work of cooperation and love. My heartfelt thanks to the women whose stories you'll read in the pages for making space in their incredible, busy lives to participate in this project. Thanks to Janet Thoma for her commitment to excellence, and to Matt Price for a heroic effort in organizing and collecting some of the material. None of this would have been possible without the self-less daily contributions of my personal assistant, Rhonda Palser. I am so thankful for my husband and children who keep my feet on the ground and my life balanced. You are such a blessing to me. And most importantly, thank You Father God for loving us enough to send the *very best*—Happy Birthday, Jesus!

Introduction

Christmas: The very word releases a flood of emotions and feelings. No other holiday so quickly stirs up memories of years gone by, all the while filling us with great anticipation for the glorious celebration that's about to begin.

The Christmas season has always been an awe-filled, family-centered event at our house. The air of anticipation begins before the first Advent candle is lit and heightens with each tradition we celebrate. I work hard at trying to establish traditions for my family. I think it gives my children a sense of heritage, and my husband and I love recalling special family memories from years past.

Christmas is also a season for the senses. Growing up with grandmothers who enjoyed baking, I loved the wonderful aromas that filled the weeks before Christmas. Passing those "kitchen treasures" on to neighbors and friends was, and still is, a special part of Christmas for me.

Most important, Christmas is a time of spiritual renewal as we celebrate the birth of our Savior. Even as a child I treasured everything about going to midnight Mass with my family on Christmas Eve because I knew it represented something wonderful and affirming. I loved bundling up and trekking into the cold winter night at an hour when I would normally have been snuggled warmly in bed. The church would be filled with the soft glow of candlelight and families reverently seated in the pews. After singing "O Holy Night" and receiving Communion, we'd all go back into the cold, dark night together, taking time to stop and enjoy the life-size manger scene under the pine trees on the church lawn. Standing in gently falling snow, we'd try to imagine the wonder of that first Christmas.

Childhood memories, special traditions, poignant moments, quiet reflections—Christmas holds different experiences and emotions for each of us. And yet, if you're like me, every Christmas I look for fresh inspiration to keep my heart and mind focused on the real "reason for the season." I believe you'll find that inspiration in this book.

Many of the women who have contributed have touched my own life—through their friendship, their music, their writing, their teaching, or their experiences. Part One, "The Memories of Christmas Past," contains memories of our childhood Christmases. Not all of us had childhoods filled with wonderful Christmases. Some have walked down very difficult paths, and you may have, as well. But all of us received God's incredible gift of forgiveness and eternal life through Jesus Christ.

Part Two, "The Memories of Christmas Present," gives our memories of later Christmases with our own families and friends. Some of these have been written specially for this book; others were first published in magazines and were especially meaningful to me.

Part Three, "Creating the Memories of Christmas Future,"

contains reminiscences that may inspire you to start a new Christmas tradition. Here we share pieces of our own special days and what they have meant to us. And finally, Part Four, "A Diary of Christmas Memories," gives you an opportunity to preserve your own Christmas traditions—for yourself and members of your family.

Though all of the women in this book enjoy the memories and traditions shared here, each of us celebrates the season with a heartfelt gratefulness to our heavenly Father for a gift beyond measure—unmerited, undeserved, yet lavishly given without reservation. Our souls sing out "Joy to the world, the Lord is come!" We pray that as we share our Christmas memories it will encourage you to "prepare Him room" in your own heart and life. And we hope you'll make this book your own, by adding *your* special memories and traditions at the end.

So sit back, throw another log on the fire, and pour a cup of hot cocoa. Take a moment to consider the real meaning of Christmas. You might want to read a selection or so from each part. Another day, just one selection. You might even read a story aloud to your family as part of your own holiday celebration.

Whether you live on a ranch in Texas or in an apartment in Minneapolis, whether you've seen winter come and go only twenty times or more than eighty, and even if you don't have a fireplace and you're allergic to chocolate, it's Christmas—the most wonderful time of the year—and we invite you to join us in reminiscing about the past, taking stock in the present, and looking forward to the future.

Merry Christmas—from our hearts to yours!

Terry Meeuwsen
Virginia Beach, Virginia

PART ONE

Christmas
Past

GLIMPSES

OF OUR

CHILDHOOD

CHRISTMASES

The Sound of Sleigh Bells

TERRY MEEUWSEN

$\mathcal{F}$or as long as I can remember, my mom and dad have gone out of their way to make Christmas a time of wonder and joy for our family. My very first Christmas memory, when I was only three, reflects the love they shared with their children by making an extra effort to delight and surprise us.

While I was still an infant my folks moved in with my mother's parents in hopes of saving enough money to make a down payment on a house. My grandparents owned an apartment building and we all lived together on the top floor.

During the Christmas season Grandma always did lots of baking. Her Norwegian cookies were a time-consuming labor of love that friends and family alike enjoyed. But as a three-year-old who had not yet developed a sophisticated sweet tooth, I was more impressed with Grandma's Christmas tree than anything that came out of her oven.

To this day I'm not sure how she was able to cover every visible patch of greenery with a dazzling and shiny ornament. I do know that her pattern never wavered. She started by lining the interior of the tree with handblown Italian glass orbs, each painted with a silver background and silhouettes of houses, bells, and birds with plumed tails. Large multicolored bulbs followed next and were strung repeatedly around and through every branch. Finally, she topped her creation off by clipping candle-shaped lights onto the pine needles that stuck through the colorful tapestry. The cylinder of each candle was filled with a liquid that bubbled and glowed in the color of the bulb that shone behind it. To say that the effect was magical to an impressionable toddler is an understatement!

I remember standing beside this brilliant display with my eyes focused on the packages nestled around the tree's base. I just knew that the doll I had hoped and prayed for was in there somewhere. She was beautiful and came with a trunk filled with the most wonderful doll clothes. I could hardly wait till Christmas morning.

My dad has always been a terrific athlete. Between basketball and baseball, he played a sport of some kind almost every weekend. Christmas Eve that year was no exception. I'm not sure what time he arrived home but he made a great deal of noise coming in and getting ready for bed. Since he was usually very quiet, I was surprised when he walked into my room and woke me up to say good night. He chatted aloud with my mother and opened and closed dressers and closet doors. When my parents were sure I was thoroughly awake, they climbed into bed and turned out the light.

Within minutes, I heard the sound of sleigh bells in the living room. *I must be imagining things!* I thought. *No, there it was again! Didn't anyone else hear it? Wasn't anyone going to get up and check?*

I slid my feet over the edge of the bed until the toes of my yellow Dr. Denton pajamas touched the floor. I first peeked into my parents' room. At that moment the bells in the living room jingled again. I jumped! But my parents never stirred. Curiosity outweighed my apprehension, and I tiptoed slowly down the hallway.

The soft glow from the Christmas tree lights made it possible for me to find my way without turning on any lights. As I moved from the hallway into the dining room I could hear rustling in the living room. Slowly, I moved to the edge of the large arched doorway that divided the two rooms and peeked around the corner. My mouth dropped open and my heart seemed to stop. *It was him!* Santa Claus was standing there admiring our tree and eating the cookies I'd left for him.

As I watched, Santa bent over and began to take packages from his bag and place them under the tree. After what seemed like an eternity, he reached in and pulled out the doll I had thought about for many long weeks. Next came the trunk of clothes that went with her.

Forgetting my fear and unable to contain my joy any longer, I gasped in delight. Santa wheeled around, feigning surprise. He leaned toward me, smiled, and winked. I don't think my feet touched the floor as I tore through the dining room and down the hallway to my bedroom. I leaped into bed, yanked the covers over my head, and lay there terrified that he would actually come into my room. I was too frightened to breathe. (I'm sure my parents were hysterical!)

At some point that evening, exhaustion overcame fear and I fell asleep. What a relief it was the next morning to find the treasured doll right where she'd been placed under the tree the night before. Years later my parents shared the identity of the mystery Santa: a friend who lived on the second floor had offered to play the part of St. Nick for several families in the building.

Our old apartment building was sold years ago and the doll is long gone, but the memory of that special Christmas Eve will be with me forever. Now that I have four children of my own, I have a new appreciation for the effort my parents took to make lasting memories for us. When money was tight or when one of them wasn't feeling well, Christmas still occurred in grand and glorious fashion. Now I'm enjoying adding my own traditions to my family's Christmas season—but not without remembering the time, effort, and love my parents invested in making every Christmas a celebration.

When it's 3:00 A.M. Christmas morning and I'm still wrapping presents and Andy, my husband, is assembling another bike, I remind myself that one day my children will be doing this while fondly remembering their own magic of Christmas past. The stories that follow reflect the happy, the sad, the surprising, but the always memorable events from holidays that are long gone but certainly not forgotten.

CHAPTER 1

Another Kind of Christmas

NAOMI JUDD

I'm fed up with Christmas! I'd bet my farm, this isn't the kind of statement you'd expect to hear from me. If you know anything about me you know how strongly I feel about my faith and my family. But, the truth is, I'm fed up with Christmas! So, if you're looking for one of those made-for-TV, "Hallmark Hall of Fame" type of Christmas stories that makes you feel warm and fuzzy, you may just as well skip over my section.

I was raised in a small town in Kentucky, the oldest of four children. My daddy was a good, honest, hardworking sort, a country boy who smoked Camels, drove a pickup truck, and ran a gas station. Mama was a housewife who lived for her husband and children.

Mama took us to the First Baptist Church each Sunday, but the Christmas pageant was one of the few occasions during the year that Daddy could be found in the pew beside us. Two weeks before Christmas, we'd all pile into our old blue station wagon and pick out a tree together. We'd string popcorn and make handmade ornaments at school to hang on the tree. We decorated the front windows of our large frame house with stencils. Every evening we would plug in the lights and open the living room drapes for people to see that we were a Christian family celebrating our most important holiday. These gestures of family bonding and affection might seem simple, but they had to satisfy my emotional craving until the following holiday season.

Christmas also brought a sweet sense of community into my life. I loved the Christmas music at school, caroling with our church group on a wintry night, and looking forward to my mother's family coming to visit from Ohio. I remember running home after school each day to read the cards and letters that had arrived in the mail. Mama would let me tape them around the doorway in our hall. Each time I walked by I would bask in the warmth of the friendships they represented.

I was always an emotional, creative, and dramatic child, and Christmas morning was no exception. I would make everyone wait at the top of the steps until Mama had gone down and put a Christmas record on the stereo. I reminded Daddy to get out the Bell-and-Howell movie camera to film our surprised faces as we marched into the living room and as we opened each present. We were a hardworking, blue-collar family, but every year Daddy and Mama made sure that each of their children got the one special gift they had hoped for that year. Mama would then serve a delicious Christmas dinner. She remains to this day the best cook I have ever known.

Perhaps you've heard the lyrics to The Judds' plaintive song, "Grandpa, Tell Me About the Good Ol' Days." If it sounds like I'm nostalgically singing for the simple pleasures of these child-hood Christmases in that song, you're right! Something dreadful has happened to Christmas. A disease has infected it, a conta-gious pathogen called *commercialism*. The symptoms of this disease are evidenced when we worship the creation, not the Creator. It has shamelessly blindsided everything we should treasure about the birth of our Savior.

A few years ago I threw a fit about what had become of Christmas in our home. I called my daughters, Wynonna and Ashley, and my husband, Larry, to a powwow at our kitchen table. I began by turning to Ashley and asking her what she was feeling about the upcoming holiday season. Ashley has always had a tender spot in her heart for the homeless; she even took time out of her busy senior year of college to volunteer regularly at a soup kitchen. She said it bothered her that some people would spend Christmas without a place to lay their heads—just like Mary and Joseph.

Wynonna mentioned that our Christian counselor had said that Christmas was her busiest time of the year because people without families feel more isolated and alone during the holidays. She told Wynonna that the suicide rate at Christmas is very high, because of the stress the season so often brings.

When Larry spoke, he recalled a conversation he had with

someone who lived in a housing project. This person said that his friends and neighbors believed that they didn't get gifts at Christmas because they had been such bad children and didn't deserve nice things.

I had heard enough! "Christmas has become a mockery of what it should be," I said. "It's the biggest retail event of the year: people go irresponsibly into debt, families are robbed of time together, and even strangers are irritable with one another because they're stuck in traffic at the mall.

"To make matters worse, the media throw implausible images of the 'perfect family' at us wherever we turn. We see pictures of models in designer clothes, sitting in a professionally decorated living room and surrounded by expensive presents. No wonder people get depressed!"

By now my family was excitedly joining me with their own observations. "Yeah, religious symbols are removed from public facilities, but prizes are given to the people who put the most lights on their house." "Have you noticed how advertisers start earlier and earlier each year?" "I hear people longing for the holidays to be over so they can stay home and relax."

"Well, I have an idea," I said with determination. "This year let's take Christmas back from the media. None of us need anything; instead let's sponsor a family from the angel tree at church. We can spend the holidays by simply enjoying one another's company, inviting family in from out of town, and calling old friends. In other words, just like Jesus, let's put other people first."

And so it began. That year we gathered a group of friends

and went to an inner-city church in Nashville, where we prepared a huge dinner for twenty-four homeless people. Afterward we sang Christmas carols, visited with our new friends, and handed out warm clothing to last through the winter. The next day we visited a center for terminally ill children and gave them presents, sang their favorite Christmas songs, and spent the afternoon playing games.

The results of our new Christmas tradition were dramatic in the Judd household. We had come together as a family and had gained new insights into the lives of others. The entire experience made us reflect on our own blessings, and we felt like we had made a tiny dent in the problems facing the world today.

I've raised both of my daughters to believe that Jesus is the Son of God and that we are to walk in His footsteps here on earth. The Christmas gift Larry and I gave Wynonna and Ashley that year was to put this belief into practice.

When we returned home on Christmas evening, we looked like anything but the "perfect designer family." But it felt more like Christmas in our home than it had in years. We had taken Christmas back and given it the honor it deserves. I pray that your family will do the same this year and experience the joyful peace of Christ's presence.

Naomi Judd

Although she would modestly insist otherwise, there has never been anything simple or commonplace about Naomi Judd—not her vision, her faith, or the music she and her daughter Wynonna created as The Judds. As their songs became number one hits, all their RCA albums went platinum and their concerts became sellouts. Their popularity kept them undefeated for eight consecutive years at all three major country awards shows. Naomi's autobiography, Love Can Build a Bridge, stayed on the New York Times best-seller list for several months and was the basis for a critically acclaimed NBC miniseries. Diagnosed in 1990 with a potentially life-threatening liver disease, Naomi declared, "The Lord is my doctor and the fans are my medicine," and she embarked on a triumphant farewell tour in 1991. Today she continues at full speed. She has opened a stylish new restaurant called Trilogy and is a highly sought after inspirational speaker whose message is one of hope, humor, and faith.

CHAPTER 2

The Kidnapped Doll

MYRTLE "COOKIE" POTTER

It was Christmas Eve and the family was gathered at my grandparents' house in San Francisco. I was six that year and my cousin Tom, eight. We'd waited for months, and now that the time for gift giving was almost near, every moment seemed a lifetime. Would I get the baby doll I longed for—the one in the window of Mrs. O'Connor's variety store? For months I'd spent part of every day staring at her with my nose pressed against the pane. I was certain that baby doll looked sad every time I left.

"Why don't they give out the presents right now?" I asked. "Why do we have to wait until after dinner?"

"I *can't* wait," said Tom. "Let's sneak into the living room. Maybe we can find out what we're getting."

"Grandpa and the uncles are out in the garden," I said. And our cousins Dorothy, Mildred, and Mabel were in the attic playing dress-up.

We peeked into the kitchen. The aroma of fresh-baked bread and roasting turkey with sage dressing filled the air. Grandma smiled as she chopped onions. Aunt Agnes and Aunt Susan bumped happily against each other as they stirred the gravy. But Aunt Margaret scowled as she basted the turkey. "You can't come in here," she said, shaking her spoon at us.

So far so good. Everyone was accounted for. We hurried down the hall to the front of the house and cautiously turned the knob on the living room door. My heart beat fast. This was forbidden territory until after dinner. We both took a deep breath and Tom pushed the door open.

What a sight! The magnificent pine tree, aglow with lights of every color, was covered with tinsel and bright ornaments. On the top an angel rested serenely, his sparkling wings brushing the ceiling.

"Wow!" whispered Tom. "Look at the presents." The rug was covered with gifts. He fell to the floor and started to shake the boxes that bore his name. "This one's just clothes, I think, but doesn't this one sound like an Erector set?"

I was too busy to answer. One of my packages smelled like perfume, another like chocolate. But where was a box that might hold a baby doll? I glanced around the room and spied something covered with a quilt behind a couch. I rushed to it and lifted the cover. Underneath was a buggy—with a doll inside. "My baby!" I cried, picking her up and hugging her.

"Put her back," hissed Tom, yanking my arm. "That doll's not yours. See, the tag says 'To Dorothy.'"

I refused to look. "She's *mine*," I insisted, jerking away. "I've wanted her forever. Santa just made a mistake putting Dorothy's name on her."

Clutching the doll, I ran down the hall and out the back door to Grandpa's workshop. Quickly I thrust the baby onto a pile of wood shavings behind a stack of lumber.

Tom came storming in after me. "You're a kidnapper and a thief," he cried. Then, losing interest, he announced he was going inside. I ran behind him. Tom's last remark worried me: "Do you think you're the only one who wanted a doll? Dorothy asked Santa for a baby too."

I hadn't thought of that. What if it really *was* hers? Her parents would be upset that the doll was missing. Tom would tell on me. Mama would be ashamed. Aunt Margaret would stare down her nose at me, just like her stuck-up daughter Dorothy.

If that doll was Dorothy's, I'd never hear the end of it. Why had I taken her? I had to put her back. My heart beating wildly, I ran as fast as I could to Grandpa's workshop and was about to open the door when I heard voices. Grandpa was in there showing Uncle Edward the cabinet he was building. I couldn't go in now.

Just then Grandma called us to dinner. Shakily I climbed the steps to the house.

In the dining room we bowed our heads as Grandpa said grace. "We thank You, Lord," he began, "for letting us all be together on the day of Jesus' birth." I almost choked. It was bad enough to be a thief and a kidnapper, but to think I'd done it all on baby Jesus' birthday!

After that I had no appetite. When our mothers finally cleared the table and started to do the dishes, I hurried back to the workshop, hoping I could get the doll. But Grandpa was in there again, this time with Uncle Archie.

When we finally gathered in the living room, my face felt hot. The party dress Mama had made me seemed too tight around my neck.

Grandpa began calling names and handing out presents. He waited for each person to open the gift before he called another name. I stole a look at Tom; he was totally involved in unwrapping his own packages. After an hour, Dorothy's buggy was still behind the couch. Though I'd received several presents, Mama could see I wasn't happy. She left the room and came back wheeling a doll buggy. "Santa left this for Myrtle," she said.

I gasped. Inside was a doll better than the one I'd taken. She had a different dress, a pretty bonnet, and a coverlet of pink and blue satin. She wore a ruffled petticoat, lace panties, and booties. I knew Mama had made them; the blanket was of the same satin she used to make Grandma a robe. My baby was so special that I hugged her tight and vowed never to let her go.

Suddenly I felt sick to my stomach. For a moment I'd forgotten Dorothy's doll. It was still missing.

"What's the matter, Myrtle?" said Mama. "Don't you like her?"

"Oh, Mama, I *love* her."

But of course, I couldn't enjoy my present until I put

Dorothy's doll back. How could I possibly do it? Jesus! It was His birthday. Maybe He could help me. *Jesus,* I prayed silently, *I'm sorry I was so bad. Please help me make things right.*

Grandpa called for attention. "We've got a lot more presents to give out. But we're going to take a recess. Pumpkin pie with whipped cream is waiting in the dining room."

This was my chance! As everyone headed for dessert, I stole out the back door and down the steps. This time no one would be in the workshop. Behind the lumber, with her dress askew and wood shavings in her hair, lay Dorothy's doll. I grabbed her and got her back to the living room without being seen. I picked the shavings out of her hair, smoothed her clothes, and started to put her in the buggy behind the couch.

But my heart sank when I saw a pink smear on her cheek. Grandpa painted landscapes and there must have been a drop of paint on the wood shavings. Rub as I might, I couldn't get it off. Dorothy and Aunt Margaret would be sure to notice it.

I knew what I had to do. With trembling fingers I undressed both dolls. I put Dorothy's doll clothes on my perfect doll, and the clothes Mama had made on the doll with the smudged cheek. I put the perfect doll in Dorothy's buggy and the one I'd kidnapped in my buggy with her smeared cheek against the pillow.

When everyone returned to the living room, Grandpa finished giving out the presents. Dorothy received her doll and was just as happy with hers as I had been with mine.

"Our dolls look like twins," I said. "Let's have a tea party for them."

"That'll be fun," said Dorothy. "I'll bring cookies."

She's not stuck-up, I told myself. *I'm sure we can be friends.*

"Mama," I said that night as I was getting into bed, "I'm naming my doll Mary, after Jesus' mother."

"That's lovely," said Mama. "You know, your doll has a little pink mark on her cheek. Mrs. O'Connor has a lot of other dolls in her store. I'm sure we can exchange her."

"No!" I cried. "I like her just the way she is."

I snuggled in my blanket, holding Mary close, filled with an overwhelming joy that had nothing to do with dolls or buggies. I was only six years old, but already I'd sensed it: When you do something bad, it's possible, with God's help, to make things right.

Cookie Potter

Cookie Potter lives in San Mateo, California. This article was originally published in Guideposts, *December 1994.*

CHAPTER 3

My Most Memorable Christmas

TWILA PARIS

*T*he heritage of the Paris family is one of service and devotion to our Lord. My earliest memories are filled with stories of relatives who have dedicated their lives to bringing the good news of salvation to a hungry world.

Perhaps this is why Christmas has always been a special time in my family. This wonderful season is an occasion when we can enjoy the support of those whose love for each other is unconditional and whose vision is blind to flaws and weaknesses. Two people I especially remember are my grandfather and grandmother Paris.

THE CARPENTER AND PASTOR

Stature is not always measured in such mundane terms as physical size or personal wealth. One of the most important and larger-than-life men I have ever known stood barely five and a half feet tall. He possessed no temporal riches—except for the countless people who considered him their friend. Yet his abundant kindness and compassion generated a spirit of love that made him seem like a giant to those whose lives he touched. That man was my grandfather Paris.

I have always felt that my grandfather's life was especially blessed because he, like our Lord, was both a pastor and a carpenter. I still remember how the same hands that could turn a pile of boards and nails into a sturdy porch or a graceful sleigh could also compose a moving sermon or baptize a new Christian.

Perhaps the most cherished memory I have of this great man happened a few weeks before one of my earliest Christmases. Over a quiet breakfast, Grandfather Paris announced in a casual way that he had an important project he needed to complete. He turned to me and explained in the sternest voice he could muster that I should remain in the house so as not to disturb him.

Well, naturally this only served to fuel my youthful imagination and curiosity. So after breakfast while everyone else scurried about, I snuck to a side window to watch Grandfather Paris as he set up his tools and materials in the backyard. It was apparent that my grandfather was indeed working on something important as he brought out the finest wood from his shed, was even more careful than usual with his measurements, and sanded and resanded after each cut.

I soon began to wonder what my grandfather could be creating that could command so much of his time and attention. It certainly didn't look very big. In fact, from my vantage point I could barely see some of the smaller boards he had finished. Surely if it were such an important project there should be more to show for his efforts than the few small items that lay on his bench.

Then, with the day wearing on (and with it, my attention), Grandfather Paris at last stood back to admire his handiwork. I'll never forget the feeling of astonishment and joy I felt when I realized that his long and patient efforts had produced the most beautiful doll's crib I had ever seen. I'll also never forget the endless days of waiting for Christmas morning when at last I could play with this wonderful present. (Believe me, patience is more than a virtue for a two-year-old. It's almost an impossibility.)

As an adult, when I think about this gesture of love from my grandfather I realize anew what it is that makes Christmas special. Just as a gentle man lovingly crafted a toy for his granddaughter to show her how very special she was to him, so, too, did God lovingly send His Son as a flawless living sacrifice to express His infinite love for us.

GRANDMOTHER PARIS'S SECRET

As a romantic gesture in honor of the first gift he gave her on their first date, my grandfather Paris always gave my grandmother Paris a box of chocolate-covered cherries for Christmas. And every year my grandmother would open her one present from my grandfather and exclaim with joy that once again she had gotten exactly what she wanted and what she had looked forward to receiving since the previous year.

My grandfather passed away before Christmas several years ago, and in an effort to help ease my grandmother's sorrow, her sons bought her a box of chocolate-covered cherries. As she had done for so many years, my grandmother opened her gift and expressed sincere appreciation for this tasty reminder of her first date. This loving exchange went on for eight years, until one day my grandmother told my sister Starla in private that she had never really cared for chocolate-covered cherries but had eaten them so as not to hurt anyone's feelings! When my father and uncle heard this revelation, they did the only honorable thing good sons could do—they continued to buy my grandmother her box of chocolate-covered cherries each Christmas.

We have since laughed many times about how my grandmother didn't express her love for her husband in such common ways as fixing grand meals or wearing his favorite perfume. Instead, she lovingly ate the one thing that made her taste buds cringe: chocolate-covered cherries.

Take time out this Christmas to show everyone in your family how much they mean to you. When you give yourself away, you offer a gift that continues to provide joy and happiness long after the needles have fallen off the tree and the sleigh bells are lying silent in the attic.

And as your family puts together a scrapbook of memories

over the years, don't forget that small things are the most important. After all, if it hadn't been for the birth of a tiny baby in a remote part of the world two thousand years ago, there would be no season in which to build our joyous remembrances.

Twila Paris

Twila Paris may sing with the ethereal transcendence of an angel, but her feet are firmly rooted in Arkansas soil. She often composes her number one radio singles while maneuvering her four-wheel-drive truck through the Ozark Mountain roads she has known since childhood. Twila's music career includes fifteen best-selling albums; more than twenty number one hits on adult contemporary, inspirational, and contemporary Christian radio; a feature performance for five years on the "Young Messiah" tours; and numerous awards, including Dove awards for Female Vocalist of the Year (1993–95), Song of the Year ("God Is in Control"), and Praise & Worship Album of the Year (Sanctuary). Twila and her husband, Jack, live in Fayetteville, Arkansas. Twila originally published this story in It's the Thought (Tyndale House), a book she cowrote with author Jeanie Price.

CHAPTER 4

A Special Christmas Moment

MADELINE MANNING MIMS

I was about ten years old when I walked the aisle of my church—Mt. Herman Baptist Church in Cleveland, Ohio—singing "O Holy Night." This Christmas moment was to be a life-changing experience for me.

I was dressed in a white robe, wore no shoes, had curly ponytails with white ribbons, and held a small microphone. I remember standing behind the closed doors of the sanctuary waiting for my cue to enter. I was so nervous, but I desperately wanted to share my love for Jesus with the congregation.

Suddenly I heard the music begin to the familiar tune that tells the story of that holy night when Jesus was born. The doors swung open, and I gingerly walked in to the beat of the music.

Halfway down the aisle, I paused and began to sing the first verse. The "oohs" and "ahs" from the congregation revealed their pleasure and approval of my rendition and displayed the effect it was having on their hearts.

Then, something *completely* unexpected happened. I felt myself leaving the sanctuary of our church! Suddenly I was transported back to that holy night when Jesus was born. I heard angels singing and I saw the manger. And in the manger, *there* was the baby Jesus!

My knees buckled and I felt myself slowly slumping to the floor in awe of this holy child. I could hear the words of the song's chorus flowing from my lips as I sang, "Fall on your knees, Oh hear the angels voices, O' night divine." I was overwhelmed by this awesome moment as the reality of Christmas flooded my being. I sang my best for this child, who was my Lord and King.

Years later I returned to Cleveland to visit some relatives. I ran into a few ladies who were at the Christmas service that night. On seeing me, they began to reminisce with excitement about my performance. One dear saint turned to her friends and said, "I'll never forget that Christmas when this chile sang 'O Holy Night.' When she fell to her knees and worshiped the Kang, I tell you, there wasn't a dry eye in the place."

I'm forty-something now, and today I still give my best for Him. He's still my Savior and King. But I'll never forget that special Christmas service when I actually knelt before Him and sang in His very presence.

Madeline Manning Mims

Named one of America's Outstanding Young Women, Dr. Madeline Manning Mims is the only American woman to win an Olympic gold medal in track for the 800-meter run. She has been a member of four Olympic teams for the United States, spanning a sixteen-year international career. As a speaker, Madeline has shared her personal testimony at the White House and is currently helping to pioneer sports ministry through the chaplaincy programs at the Olympic games and other international events. She has an honorary doctorate from Oral Roberts University and heads a ministry, Ambassadorship, Inc., with her family in Tulsa, Oklahoma.

CHAPTER 5

The Best Christmas Present Ever

KIM ALEXIS DUGUAY

*W*hen I look back at all of my childhood Christmases, I think of my family and traveling to see all of my relatives who lived two hours away.

I grew up outside of Buffalo, New York, so we always had white Christmases. All of the relatives would hang around inside the house, playing games or watching television. We did need to brave the cold for an occasional walk because we ate too much.

We would also have Christmas at our house before the actual holiday with just my parents, my sister, Rhonda, and I. My mother would color-code our presents, using different wrapping paper and no bows and put them in stacks. She was a very good shopper (and still is), and we got a lot of clothes. We never were able to read her Christmas shopping lists because she wrote them in shorthand; I never did learn that in school!

After our early Christmas was done, we hopped in the car, which was packed with presents and clothes, and we were off to our grandparents' houses. We would spend Christmas Eve with my mother's parents because my grandmother is Swedish. She arrived in this country by boat when she was sixteen. The Swedish celebrate much of their holiday on Christmas Eve. That was a wonderful time for eating Swedish meatballs, Swedish raw fish with cream, and turkey. My grandmother would say the Lord's Prayer in Swedish, and I can still remember that prayer—it's the only Swedish I know.

Then it came time for the presents. My mother had only one sister, and I was fifteen before I had a cousin, so it was really just Rhonda and I as the kids. We had a blast opening all of the presents and really thought we were getting away with something great; we had three separate Christmases, and one of them was on Christmas Eve.

Christmas *Day* would finally come, and we would leave my mother's parents, drive twenty minutes to my father's parents, and start all over. We had four cousins our age on my father's side so there was always a lot of kid confusion and activity, more presents opened (What a mess!) and then another great meal.

I remember having to always sit at the "kids' table." Since I was the oldest grandchild, I was always put in charge of them all. Some years we would go play in the snow with our cousins and have snowball fights, make snowmen, and play in the creek that ran by my grandparents' house. We would always come in cold and wet and be greeted by a warm house, warm family, and warm homemade cookies.

I look back on my childhood Christmases as a time of security and happiness (and being well fed!). One of my favorite memories, though, was of going to midnight Christmas Eve services at the church and singing "O Holy Night" as silent, soft snow blanketed our words as they soared toward heaven. That was always special to me because I felt so close to God and knew I was right where I was supposed to be—in church, thanking Jesus for being born and thanking God for giving us His only Son to save us from our sins. Even with three separate Christmases, this was the best present of all!

Kim Alexis Duguay

Kim Alexis Duguay, whose face has graced the covers of more than five hundred magazines around the world, is one of America's leading supermodels. She is now beginning to make as much of an impact on television and radio as she has in the modeling world. Her broadcasting career includes three years as fashion editor of Good Morning America. *She hosts two cable shows—*Healthy Kids *on the Family Channel and* Ticket to Adventure with Kim Alexis *on the Travel Channel—and is the host of a radio feature called "Bet You Didn't Know That."*

She and her husband, Ron, reside in southern California with their five children.

CHAPTER 6

The Babies of Christmas

LEE EZELL

---

*E*ven though the warm California sun would prevent a white Christmas, I knew the Yuletide was fast approaching. I put my hands on my big belly, knowing I'd never enjoy even one Christmas with the baby I was carrying. I could relate to Mary—an unwed, pregnant teenager who pondered many things in her heart.

Christmases growing up in Philadelphia's inner city were cold in more ways than one. My four sisters and I dreaded the opening of stockings on Christmas morning, knowing the one who behaved the worst during the year would receive a lump of coal in the bottom.

But after all, what could we expect? We were mistakes, weren't we? Our father had told us repeatedly he wanted sons, not daughters. And here we were, five mistakes born to alcoholic parents who were struggling to find meaning in their own lives.

One holiday season, when I was seventeen, I found myself looking for a few laughs at something called a Billy Graham Crusade. I improved more than my sense of humor that night. I went forward and received the incorruptible seed of Christ in my life—a seed that would later grow into a great, strong oak tree.

Shortly after graduating from high school, I moved with my mother and sisters to the West Coast, leaving my father behind in Philadelphia to his life on the streets. I landed my first job in San Francisco. At last I felt I had a fresh start. How could I have imagined that soon—as a teenage virgin and a brand-new Christian—I would be raped by a man at work. This traumatizing event was only compounded when I discovered that the rape had resulted in pregnancy.

After revealing the situation to my mother, she begged me to leave home and come back when it was all over. The only stabilizing influence in my life was the Savior who dwelt within me.

As I desperately searched the Scriptures for direction, I discovered the beautiful prayer of King David in Psalm 139. His powerful words convinced me that the baby I carried was a child of God—a child who had a right to live:

> *For You formed my inward parts;*
> *You covered me in my mother's womb. . . .*

My frame was not hidden from You,
When I was made in secret.

Based on these verses I realized for the first time that I was not, in reality, an unwanted child. I also knew that the baby I was carrying was infinitely valuable too. After all, God never consults parents for their permission to create a baby. And if it is God who decides conception, then there can be no such thing as an illegitimate child.

I decided that abortion was a permanent solution to a temporary problem. *Surely I can find a way to go full term with this pregnancy*, I thought. Even though I had not volunteered for this baby, I decided that no mother really makes this choice. A couple decides when to make love, but God decides when to create life. With one notable exception, no unborn child asks to come into the world. Jesus Christ was the only One!

In Los Angeles I found a loving Christian family who took me in and gave me the support I needed during my pregnancy. Shortly after Christmas, the only child I would ever bear was born in a Los Angeles county hospital, a baby girl whom I never held or saw. Adoption papers were signed, and I entrusted my baby to the One "who is able to keep that which we commit to Him." In California, adoption records are sealed. I knew this would be a closed chapter in my life.

Ironically, ten Christmases later, I found myself on the other side of the adoption experience. In a Los Angeles courthouse I adopted two beautiful daughters, Pam and Sandi. I had married their father, Hal Ezell, after his wife, the birthmother of his two little girls, had died. Now God was giving me the assignment of being their mother.

Soon I became convinced that motherhood involves more than carrying a child for nine months. I gained a new love and understanding for adoptive parents. Over the years I never thought of myself as an "unnatural" mother (vs. a "natural" parent) or an "unreal" mother (vs. someone who is "real"). Both mothers had divine assignments in the lives of these precious girls. In considering my own birthdaughter, I certainly hoped she would call her mother *Mom*, just as I was glad when my own adopted daughters did the same. Each Christmas I couldn't help thinking of Joseph, who had the very awesome responsibility of serving as the adopted father to God's only Son!

Ten more Christmases passed. One December day I was sitting at home, pulling out Christmas decorations, when the phone rang. The voice on the other end of the line announced, "Hello, you've never met me, but you're my mother." My heart nearly stopped and my mouth dried up.

This voice named Julie went on to explain her motivation for finding me. She wanted to let me know I was a grandmother! And, more important, she wanted to achieve a dream she had always had: to lead her birthmother to Christ. After silently listening to her attempts at evangelism, I finally had to interrupt her. "Julie," I stumbled, "I think you are trying to lead me to Christ, but you already did that many years ago." We both began to cry.

The first time I laid eyes on my daughter, she walked through the door and passed me her baby, saying, "Now, you go to your grandma." Her big husband, Bob Makimaa, anxiously awaited his turn to stretch out his arms and say, "Lee, I want to thank you for not aborting Julie. What would I do without her and our children?"

Our tearful reunion convinced us of one thing: God is faithful, and He is truly able to make all things work together for our good. When Julie discovered that she was conceived through rape, she had quite a struggle. But her pastor showed her many Scripture passages that would convince her she was the product of love—God's love. She later remarked, "If Psalm 139 is true, then it was God who wanted me to be born." I couldn't agree with her more.

We talked about her adoptive parents, Harold and Eileen Anderson. Their openness with adoption information made Julie's search a successful one. With the restoration of this missing piece in the puzzle from my past, all of our lives were permanently changed!

Julie's adoptive mom came to Los Angeles with Julie one Mother's Day and the two of us, two mothers sharing one daughter, held a press conference. Along with Julie, we later told the heartwarming details of our lives in my book *The Missing Piece* (Servant Publications). My goal was to give hope to others who may not realize that God is working behind the scenes to right the wrongs of life, and make sense out of our nonsense.

At this writing, ten more years have passed, and I've just had the first Christmas when "all my children" could coordinate a celebration together: Pam, Sandi, and Julie along with my three grandchildren, Casey, Herb, and Mason. We are an odd blended family, but we relish the joys of the season, understanding that "the hopes and fears of all our years" are met in Christ today.

God used our reunion to make His point about the origin of life, and we found ourselves challenged to share that story on various television talk shows. Julie always stirred the emotions of those who were watching when she would boldly state, "I am so glad I did not get the death penalty for the crime committed by my father."

Lee Ezell

Lee Ezell has come a long way since growing up in Philadelphia's inner city, the child of alcoholic parents. Today she is a wife, mother, and author who speaks at schools, seminars, and churches of all denominations. Her best known book is The Missing Piece, which tells of the daughter she gave up for adoption and their reunion years later.

CHAPTER 7

A Wartime Christmas

ANNA HAYFORD

The year was 1941 and Pearl Harbor had been attacked only a few weeks before. To an eight-year-old girl, the full impact could hardly be realized. My two oldest brothers had already enlisted and would be going into the U. S. Marine Corps right after Christmas. But the anticipation of the festivities just ahead was uppermost in my mind.

Our family was busy with normal holiday preparations—baking, shopping, decorating. There were also the rehearsals for the children's program at church, which was held on Christmas Eve. We all had our little readings or songs to learn, so the impending separation of some of our family members did not register with me.

There were nine children in my family, so we never lacked for a playmate. Of course, living on a farm we had lots of chores and work to do and were kept quite busy with regular duties. Everyone helped!

Daddy had a heart condition that prevented him from holding a regular job, so our family was sustained mainly by welfare. I can remember going with my mother to stand in line and receive government surplus items that helped feed our large family.

Because of the financial limitations in our home, none of the gifts we received for Christmas were very costly; many times they were secondhand or homemade items. My siblings and I always managed to get some kind of gift for each other, though. They may have only cost five cents, but we enjoyed them and were thankful for the things we received.

My poor mother got more hot pads and Evening in Paris cologne than she could possibly use, while Daddy's gifts were bandanna handkerchiefs or sleeve holders. I usually received things like little wire bracelets or hair ribbons.

Christmas Eve was my favorite holiday celebration. Early in the evening a local missions group, Job's Daughters, would come by our home and leave baskets of the most wonderful goodies imaginable. Daddy's doctor was a sponsor of this charitable group of young women and he made sure we were remembered every year.

The eyes of the younger children in the family would grow to the size of silver dollars as we surveyed the baskets that contained everything from fresh vegetables to candy and gifts.

My mother would never let us "dive" right in, but that's what we wanted to do. I cannot put into words what a blessing these gifts were to our family.

We didn't own a car so we walked to and from church, which was about a half mile from our house. December on the plains of Nebraska is very cold. As we walked home from church that Christmas Eve, we were dressed from head to toe in the warmest clothes we could find. We all wore our coats, mittens, scarves, boots, and caps and felt quite snug in spite of the subzero temperatures.

The moon was full and bright, and we watched for the dancing of the Northern Lights as we walked through the crunching snow. Huge cottonwood trees stood as leafless sentinels on the east side of the road while the other side was one snow-covered field after another. It was a simple time in our lives, but a happy one. In between carol singing, we'd talk about opening gifts when we arrived home or plan what we would eat for dinner—a subject very important to a family of six boys!

As I mentioned before, the children's program was always on Christmas Eve. Our Sunday school was small enough that after the songs and skits, each child's name was called to go up front to receive a gift. We were always excited to get the presents, but we also enjoyed the boxes of candy donated by the church and the huge popcorn balls made by one of the elderly ladies in our congregation.

Because of the size of our family and because of all the things we received, my father always took a fifty-pound flour sack to church on Christmas Eve to haul our "loot" home. We enjoyed seeing our dad look like our own private Santa Claus as he threw that sack over his shoulder.

Needless to say, after all that excitement, we certainly weren't ready to go to bed and wait for Santa when we got home. That year we unanimously decided to open our gifts on Christmas Eve. After all the gifts were opened and we had time to play with some of our "new" things, Mama scooted us all off to bed. We had had a lovely Christmas Eve with *everyone* home.

Christmas morning was the beginning of another thrilling day and our house was full of activity. As a child, I never saw a Christmas without snow, which afforded us all kinds of fun things to do. The North Platte River was on the back of our property and we loved to ice-skate. In addition we played Fox and Geese, made angels in the snow, and went sledding. We played until it was too cold to stay out any longer. The warmth of the house was so inviting with the smell of dinner cooking and Daddy cracking hazelnuts for us. We promptly filled up on nuts and candy while we worked on a jigsaw puzzle.

I have tried to give you a feeling of what our Christmases were like fifty-five years ago. As I think back on those wonderful memories, it causes me to reflect on the Christmases I enjoy today.

Many things have changed in my home. Instead of homemade decorations, we have purchased or received some very lovely ornaments. We love everything about the holidays: the decorations, the giving and receiving of gifts, the carols, the Christmas story, and the church programs. Instead of the very inexpensive presents my family gave when I was a child, we are now able to exchange far nicer gifts. Instead of walking through the snow (which I still miss), we live in southern California where the weather never gets terribly cold.

But in spite of the things that have changed, what I have come to realize and understand is that the true joy of Christmas has nothing to do with the *things* that make up the holiday celebrations. It all comes back to the *people* who do the celebrating. Even if a person is able to give expensive gifts and hold elaborate banquets, if you have no one to share this abundance with, then all the joy is gone.

Yes, 1941 was a very good year for my family. We didn't realize then that all nine of us children wouldn't be together again in one place for fifty-one years. On December 26 we placed a small banner with two stars on it in the front window of our house. It stayed there until my brothers returned home safely from the war. We added another star a year later when one more brother entered the military. Until 1992 other circumstances kept us apart as a group, but our love for one another never diminished.

The stars in our window reminded us that we had brothers serving our country and that they were living far from home. The star of Bethlehem, which introduced Christmas to the world, not only let us know that the Messiah was alive, but that we can have new life through Him—and life more abundantly.

Anna Marie Hayford

Anna Marie Hayford was the seventh child born into the Nebraska family of Elmer and Emma Smith. Having been raised in a godly home, she received Jesus as her Savior at an early age. Today she and her husband, Pastor Jack Hayford, have been married for almost forty-five years and have four children and nine grandchildren. In 1969, after many years of ministry in the Foursquare Gospel Church, she and Jack felt called to take a small church in Van Nuys, California. That congregation, The Church on the Way, has grown from eighteen people to over eight thousand members. A marvelous chef, she has compiled two cookbooks, Anna's Favorites, Volumes 1 and 2, a collection of recipes her family and friends have enjoyed through the years.

CHAPTER 8

The Simple Pleasures of Christmas

JEANIE MATHEWS PRICE

*M*y father has been a minister for almost forty years. When I was a little girl we didn't have a lot of material possessions, but our home was filled with love and laughter and the abiding richness of God's presence.

I remember one Christmas when we lived in Ottumwa, Iowa, where my father was the pastor of the First Church of the Nazarene. As usual my sister and I eagerly awaited the festivities and traditions of the season: reading the Christmas story, the Christmas Eve candlelight service, getting that one special gift we had been dropping hints about since the middle of summer.

That year, however, my mother decided to treat us with a little something extra. I'll never forget the snowy morning when she left early to go shopping and brought home a large cardboard box that contained what would become a cherished family memory. It wasn't a sled or a bicycle or an oversized dollhouse. In fact, it was the last thing we expected.

Inside that big brown box were more pieces of cardboard—only these were gaily colored and looked like . . . bricks. Yes, bricks. And underneath were cardboard logs, and a cardboard mantel, and, finally, cardboard fire! Our small parsonage was filled with the warmth of the holidays, but it was missing, my mother decided, that one attribute that was featured on the cover of almost every Christmas card, holiday catalog, and seasonal book: a fireplace. And now we had one too!

My father quickly attached each piece and soon we were sitting beside a roaring 40-watt lightbulb. The glow it cast on our smiling faces reflected the peace and contentment we felt in our hearts, knowing that we were warm and safe inside a home filled with happiness and love.

That was over two decades ago, and the Lord has since blessed each member of my family in ways that we could not then have imagined. Yet when I think back over memorable events in my life, it is always the simple pleasures that stand out. Simple pleasures like that first evening when my family sat around our new fireplace and enjoyed just being together. It may have only cost a few dollars and has long since fallen apart, but its value has been immeasurable and its impact timeless in terms of the memories it created.

Today I repeatedly hear people say that they would be happy if only they had a more prestigious job or if they just owned a nicer car or if next year they could afford to go to an exotic island on their vacation. Sadly, I even hear comments like this from men and women who sit in church pews each Sunday and who hold in their hands the secrets to eternal peace and happiness: the holy Word of God.

As a child my mother gave our family a simple Christmas gift that was significant because of the love it represented. As an adult the single most important gift that my heavenly Father offers me—on Christmas or any other day—is the pleasure of a holy life in His presence.

Jeanie Mathews Price

Few people who receive a degree in philosophy go on to have careers as inspirational writers. But Jeanie Price brings her talents as a precise and logical thinker to the craft of devotional writing and the seven books she has published, including It's the Thought *(Tyndale House) and the best-selling* The Gift of Love *(Star Song). She is a frequent speaker who focuses on issues of marriage and family. Jeanie, her husband, Matthew, and daughter, Savannah, live in Nashville, Tennessee.*

CHAPTER 9

The Language of Love

JUNE HUNT

Hope deferred makes the heart sick,
But when the desire comes, it is a
    tree of life.

Proverbs 13:12

When I was twelve, my parents were gone for many months on a business trip to the Middle East. So during the Christmas holidays, my brother, two sisters, and I traveled to our grandmother's house in Idabel, Oklahoma.

Naturally, we children looked forward to our Christmas presents with great excitement. This particular year my one and only request was for, of all things, a football.

I wanted a football so badly, I thought of nothing else. My

brother Ray and I, along with cousins Tom and Ken, made a fearsome foursome. We played Monopoly, dominoes, baseball, and games of all kinds—including football. Because I was the youngest, the smallest, and the only girl, if anyone was left out, naturally it would be me. I couldn't run as fast or throw as far as the boys on our little team. Perhaps having my own football would make me a better player, and maybe then I'd be more accepted.

My grandmother didn't see my insecurity and I never spoke of it. Thinking a football wasn't feminine, she hinted at other "girl gifts" that I might like instead. She offered a variety of games and gadgets, but I was resolute in my one request. I still wanted that football!

Just before Christmas Eve, I stole a peek beneath the tree, hoping to spy my present. But what I *didn't* find made my heart sink. It wasn't there. The message was clear: Regardless of my longing, a football wasn't a gift for a girl. Although I didn't know Scripture then, I well understood the pain of Proverbs 13:12: "Hope deferred makes the heart sick."

When Christmas Eve came, I tried to be happy. Then it was time for "the tree." The colorful collection underneath the branches had grown bigger. Although I was handed a box big enough to hold a football, I also knew it could easily contain a stuffed dog, a frilly dress, or, even worse, a sissy doll (ugh!). I held my breath, broke the bow, and peeled the paper. Immediately fireworks went off in my heart: It was my football! Granny hadn't forgotten. My heart was important to her. I held the proof in my hands.

In time, I grew up and no longer needed to prove myself to the guys. While my desire for a football has waned, I'll never lose the tender affection for a grandmother who heard the longing in my heart and spoke my language of love.

More expensive gifts have found their way underneath my tree, but none have been more memorable. While a critic may cry, "You spoil people if you give them gifts which they pick out themselves." Yet how many presents have you received that weren't meaningful, much less memorable? Too many gifts are set to the side, simply collecting cobwebs.

The lesson of that long ago Christmas has remained throughout my life: *Am I hearing the hearts of others?* Now, when I give gifts, I first try to understand *their* "language of love." Since I'm on the lookout for thoughtful gifts all year long, I've found it can be great fun!

For example, a few years ago at the Texas State Fair, I came upon the perfect presents for many members of my family. A booth that sold unique sweatshirts caught my attention. Emblazoned on the front of one sweatshirt was a large, pink pig . . . *with wings!* This creation was called "Pigasus," an obvious takeoff on the mythological flying horse, Pegasus. Since my sister-in-law, Nancy, adores pigs, it was perfect for her.

My thoughts next turned to my sister Helen, who had recently received her master's degree in art history. On her sweatshirt was Pigcasso—a pig painting with an oil palette in one hoof. How perfect. My next choice was for my sister Swanee, named after Aunt Swann, who married Charles Lake (get it—Swan Lake!). Both she and Aunt Swann received sweatshirts with pigs gracefully ice-skating on "Swine Lake." And Mother, who had just started going to the Aerobic Center, could now exercise in style with the "Aeropigs," a herd of swine energetically working out in their sweatsuits. My final find was for Ray, the teller of tales about Big Foot. In honor of this legendary creature, he received a porker named "Pig Foot."

The swine sweatshirts were a huge hit. Despite the appearance of being silly gifts, these handpicked presents have been remembered for many Christmases. The personalized pigs made an impression not just because of their humor, but because they reflected the interest of each family member.

In all of our gift giving, we can double the joy of others: First, our loved ones will know we're really willing to speak their language of love, and second, they will enjoy the gift so much more than a mere perfunctory present . . . even if that gift is as unconventional as a little girl's football.

> *Let each of you look out not only*
> *for his own interests,*
> *but also for the interests of others. (Phil. 2:4)*

June Hunt

June Hunt defies the adage, "You can't be in two places at the same time." Her award-winning radio program, "Hope for the Heart," is heard daily across the nation, giving God's principles for to-

day's problems. She is also a successful speaker, singer, and author. Her books include the devotional Seeing Yourself Through God's Eyes *and* Healing the Hurting Heart. *As a musician, June has appeared on NBC's* Today Show, *toured with the USO, and been a guest soloist for the Billy Graham Crusades. Her three albums—*The Whisper of My Heart, Hymns of Hope, *and* Songs of Surrender—*reflect her message of hope: God mends the broken heart when you give Him all the pieces.*

PART TWO

THE MEMORIES OF

Christmas

Present

GLIMPSES

OF

LATER YEARS

There are only two lasting bequests
we can give our children —
one is roots, the other, wings.

Roots and Wings

TERRY MEEUWSEN

$\mathscr{I}$ have a framed quote, beautifully rendered by a calligrapher, hanging in the hall outside our children's bedrooms. It reads, "There are only two lasting bequests we can give our children: One is roots and the other is wings."

I believe that giving our children roots—a sense of who they are and what their family stands for—provides them with the wings they need to fly upward and onward toward the great potential God has given them. Of course, establishing roots requires not only time and energy; it also demands consistency and endurance. You don't put down roots by running a sprint— we're talking a Boston Marathon here.

Keeping holiday traditions sometimes requires the same tenacity. At Christmastime our house becomes a holiday wonderland. Snow villages, wreaths, candles, garlands, and bows adorn tabletops, mantels, and doors. Christmas music plays twenty-four hours a day. Anything on our property that happens to be red and green is displayed. And then, as if there isn't enough chaos in the house already, there are costumes needed for the school play and packages to be mailed to family and friends. I'm getting tired just writing about it!

Yet, I know my family loves and looks forward to every minute of it—and so do I. I'd be lying to you, however, if I didn't admit there have been some years when pulling it all together has seemed pretty overwhelming. Have you ever started a tradition and then had second thoughts about making it happen all over again, event after event, year after year?

Some of our family traditions are just for fun, like the Dutch observance of filling stockings on December 5. Did you know that tradition revolved around Ol' St. Nick's desire to help people in need?

St. Nicholas was actually a Christian pastor, the bishop of Myra in Lycea, an important seaport of the early Christian centuries. He grew up in a godly home, and his family was well to do. It seemed to be Nicholas's good pleasure to give his inheritance away to the needy. One of the most well-known legends of his life tells of a poor man who was unable to provide dowries for his three daughters. Without dowries, they were unable to marry and would be forced into a life of slavery. Upon hearing of the family's predicament, Nicholas took a sack of gold and tossed it into the family's house through the window. (Some versions say it was thrown down the chimney.) So we hang our stockings on the evening of the fifth, hoping that in the night an anonymous "giver" will fill them with candy, fruit, nuts, and small gifts.

Many of our traditions are significant observances of our Christian faith and they actually refresh my spirit during the pandemonium of the season. The lighting of the Advent wreath is one of my favorites. Each year we start with four fresh candles. A figure of baby Jesus lies in the center of the wreath. Small samplings of gold, frankincense, and myrrh are set before the figure to remind us that He is our King and we are to present our hearts to Him. One of our children lights the appropriate Advent candle and another reads from an Advent devotional. My husband, Andy, usually reads a Scripture or a Christmas meditation followed by a time of family prayer. A third child then picks a "surprise" felt piece from the pocket of our Advent calendar and places it in its appropriate spot. Finally, a fourth child blows out the candles. Each night we rotate, so that every one of our children has a chance to do each activity.

Sometimes this is a quiet, meaningful, reflective time. Often, however, it is filled with the movement of antsy children, inappropriate giggles, and bickering. Nonetheless, I am learning to trust God to speak to my children's hearts. My job is to provide the opportunity—in season and out—for my family to celebrate Jesus. It is the Holy Spirit's job to make it take hold in their hearts.

I try to sprinkle our holidays with traditions that encourage our time together and define who we are as Christians. Whether we're baking a birthday cake for Jesus or hanging handmade ornaments on the tree, it's often the times that we stop running and just enjoy each other that I treasure the most.

There have been situations when I've wondered if my effort is worth the trouble. Then, just when I feel like giving up, the Lord sends a moment of encouragement to help me "press on toward the goal."

One incident really encouraged me. I had always been fascinated by the feasts of the Old Testament. One spring I decided we should celebrate Passover as a family. I went about gathering all that I would need for a traditional Passover meal—matzo, a lamb shank, bitter herbs, etc. The table was set with our loveliest china, and I had prepared the appropriate Scriptures and prayers for each person. I had such high hopes for an evening that would really be meaningful to my family.

The Passover celebration is meant to be a leisurely time together. Well, my children eat with one foot under the table and the other one pointed in the direction they intend to go when they have swallowed their last bite. By the end of the meal I wondered what had possessed me to attempt this. As the last prayer was uttered my children whined, "*Now* can we please be excused?"

After they had left, Andy looked at me from the other end of the table. Understanding my frustration, he asked with kindness in his voice, "Why do you do this to yourself?"

"I have no earthly idea," I said, sighing. I was so discouraged.

That night as I was putting Tyler, our youngest, to bed, I began to give him the blessing I give each of our children when we pray at night. "I sign Tyler with the sign of Jesus' cross. I cover him with the blood of the Lamb of God . . ."

Suddenly, he shot up in bed. "Hey Mom, I'm just like the doorpost from the Passover!"

I hugged him. "Oh Tyler. You got it! You actually got it!"

Remembering that moment encourages me when I don't feel like I want to "keep on keeping on" with my family traditions.

In the middle of holiday activities, when it would be so easy to let these things slide, I remind myself that I don't do these things because I *have* to. I do them because I *want* to provide moments that may shape my children in years to come.

Pope Paul VI wrote, "Every mother is like Moses. She does not enter the promised land. She prepares a world she will not see." For every one of us who endeavors to make "spiritual moments" happen for our families, Galatians 6:9 is a wonderful word of encouragement: "And let us not grow weary while doing good, for in due season we shall reap if we do not lose heart."

The stories that follow are by women who have been inspired to create the spirit of Christmas in the lives of those around them. Their willingness to share Christ's message of love and hope has encouraged friends, family members, and strangers alike. While the circumstances they share are different, their message is consistent: When you give of yourself, the returns far outweigh the investment.

CHAPTER 10

Hark, the Herald Silverhawks

DALE HANSON BOURKE

*I*t's going to be Christmas very soon now," Claire announced from the backseat in her best motherly voice. As the oldest and most mature member of our car pool, she often took it upon herself to remind the other children of an upcoming event.

Buckled into their seats after an active day at school, the rest of the children squirmed and squealed and talked over one another in excited tones.

"We're going to have the biggest Christmas tree in the whole world," declared David.

"I'm going to get a hundred million toys," my son said.

"We're going to decorate our house with beautiful, beautiful stars," Claire added.

I listened to their conversation and tried to keep from interrupting. I had learned that letting the children interact naturally in this strange little world of our car pool gave me new insights into their thinking, for better or for worse. Except for occasionally refereeing a dispute, I mostly listened to the discussion as the children reviewed the day's events with all of the drama that four-year-olds could muster.

But as the conversation continued I began to have an uneasy feeling that the children were missing out on the true meaning of the upcoming holiday. "Does anyone know whose birthday it is?" I asked.

"Jesus'!" they all said in unison. I felt relieved as they began to tell their versions of Christ's birth.

"There were camels and sheeps and everything there," my son Chase explained earnestly, "and He was born in a—"

"Manger," Claire chimed in.

Reclaiming his platform, Chase raised his voice. "And then beautiful fairies came to see baby Jesus."

"Fairies?" I asked.

"Yes," my son said emphatically. "Beautiful fairies. And they told the sheep men to come."

"Don't you mean angels?" I suggested.

"Nope," my son said, shaking his head. "Fairies."

I groaned as I began to question my son's spiritual education. Where had I gone wrong? Maybe I'd told him too many imaginary tales at bedtime instead of reading a Bible storybook. Perhaps he spent too much time coloring in his Sunday school class. Whatever had gone wrong, I was determined to change things before he turned into a total secular humanist.

The next day I went to the store to buy a manger. I passed by all of the beautiful china and crystal figures and settled on an inexpensive straw-covered manger and unbreakable plastic figurines. I wanted four-year-old fingers to be able to caress the baby Jesus, to relive the coming of the wise men. I wanted to teach that Christ was approachable. It seemed like such a perfect opportunity to bring the spiritual world to life.

After school I invited Claire to join Chase and me in setting up our manger. The two of them seemed delighted to be having a "manger party," and as I began to set the stage for the story of Christ's birth, I felt that a special moment was about to occur.

I had just explained that Mary and Joseph were far away from home when Chase said, "Just a minute. I have to get something." I heard him shuffling through his toy box in the other room. After a minute he returned with his plastic igloo and toy Eskimos, which he carefully placed next to the manger. "The Eskimos wanted to see baby Jesus too," he explained.

"But there weren't any Eskimos when Jesus was born," I said. "Yes there were!" Chase said. "They ate fish and used sleds," he said deliberately, trying to teach me the lessons he had learned at school.

I decided there wasn't anything terribly sacrilegious about the Eskimos seeing baby Jesus, so I let them stay. I launched back into the story patiently. Then Chase's face lit up as he had another idea.

"Wait a minute, Mom," he said and ran off once again. He

came back with his Silverhawk, a half-human toy I'd always found disgusting.

"He can help the fairies tell everybody about Jesus," he said excitedly.

That was too much. "Just a minute. There were *angels*, not *fairies*, remember? And there certainly weren't Silverhawks." Chase was too busy dive-bombing the manger to listen.

Claire, who had been patiently putting up with Chase, sided with me. "Well, I'm going to help put the shepherds and the animals in the little house," she said.

"No, I am," Chase said competitively.

"You can have the wise men," Claire offered. "But I get Mary and baby Jesus."

"Mom! It's my house, so I get baby Jesus, right?" Chase said, his voice rising with emotion.

"No, I said it first, so I get him," Claire said, standing her ground.

Before I could intervene, Chase and Claire were locked in battle over baby Jesus.

"Hold it," I said loudly, losing my patience. I began to pry them apart.

Chase, who had wrestled control of the Jesus figure, threw it across the room and in a fit of temper yelled, "I don't care about dumb old baby Jesus anyway. I'd rather play with my Silverhawk."

By then we were all beginning to cry. Not only had I failed in my attempts at explaining the true significance of Christmas,

I had set the stage for what seemed to be the most appalling display of sacrilege I had ever seen.

I sent Chase to his room, escorted Claire home, and returned to the scene of the crime to see if I could gain any spiritual understanding from the mess. I looked at the figures on the floor, the igloo on the table, and the Silverhawk still perched atop the manger, and despite my frustration, I began to laugh. I had wanted so much to make Christ's birth real to my son. And the nativity scene in our family room was certainly more real than any other I had seen.

Just then Chase walked back into the room hesitantly. "I'm sorry that I threw baby Jesus," he said. "Can we tell the story now about the shepherds and the wise men and the fai—, I mean angels?"

With his tearstained face and sheepish grin, Chase was beginning to look like an angel again himself. As I told him the story of Christmas, he carefully placed the figures in their respective places. Then he said softly, "Is it all right if my Sky Commander comes to see baby Jesus too?"

"Sure," I said.

Over the next few days I found many other toys and stuffed animals surrounding our manger, all facing the baby Jesus, some even bearing gifts. There was something deeply moving about this strange little scene in our family room. It wasn't at all what I'd had in mind when I set out to create a spiritual experience for my son. But somehow I didn't think Jesus would mind.

Dale Hanson Bourke

Dale Hanson Bourke is publisher of Religion News Service, a division of Newhouse News Service, and a nationally syndicated columnist. Author of four books, her latest projects include The Passages of Life Bible *(Nelson) and* Turn Toward the Wind *(Zondervan). Her writing has appeared in several national magazines, including* Reader's Digest, New Woman, Guideposts, *and* The Saturday Evening Post. *She has served on the board of directors of World Vision, an international relief and development organization, and is active in her church and community. Dale lives just outside Washington, D.C., with her husband and two sons.*

CHAPTER 11

A Song for Elizabeth

ROBIN COLE

*D*ecember snow swept across the parking lot of Crescent Manor Convalescent Home. As the youngest nurse on staff, I sat with the charge nurse at the north wing station, staring out the double-glass doors and waiting for the first wave of evening visitors. At the sound of bedroom slippers flapping against bare heels, I turned to see Elizabeth, one of our patients, striding down the corridor.

"Oh, please," groaned the charge nurse, "not tonight! Not when we're shorthanded already!"

Rounding the corner, Elizabeth jerked the sash of her tired chenille robe tighter around her skinny waist. We hadn't combed her hair for a while, and it made a scraggly halo around her wrinkled face.

"Doop doop," she said, nodding quickly and hurrying on. "Doop doop," she said to the man in the dayroom slumped in front of the TV, a belt holding him in his wheelchair.

The charge nurse turned to me. "Can you settle her down?"

"Shall I go after her or wait till she comes around again?"

"Just wait. I may need you here before she gets back. She never does any harm. It's just that ridiculous sound she makes. I wonder if she thinks she's saying words!"

A group of visitors swept through the front doors. They came in, scraping feet on the rug, shaking snow from their coats, cleaning their glasses. They clustered around the desk, seeking information, and as they did Elizabeth came striding by again. "Doop doop," she said happily to everyone. I moved out to intercept the purposeful strider.

"Elizabeth," I said, taking her bony elbow, "I need you to do something for me. Come and sit down and I'll tell you about it." I was stalling. This wasn't anything I had learned in training, but I would think of something.

The charge nurse stared at me and, shaking her head, turned her attention to the group of visitors surrounding the desk. Nobody ever got Elizabeth to do anything. We counted it a good day if we could keep her from pacing the halls.

Elizabeth stopped. She looked into my face with a puzzled frown. "Doop doop," she said.

I led her to a writing table in the dayroom and found a piece of paper and a pencil. "Sit down here at the desk, Elizabeth. Write your name for me."

Her watery eyes grew cloudy. Deep furrows appeared between her brows. She took the stubby pencil in her gnarled hand and held it above the paper. Again and again she looked at the paper and then at me questioningly.

"Here. I'll write it first, and then you can copy it, okay?"

In large, clear script, I wrote ELIZABETH GOODE.

"There you are. You stay here and copy that. I'll be right back."

At the edge of the dayroom I turned, half expecting to see her following me, but she sat quietly, pencil in hand. The only sound now came from the muffled voices of visitors and their ailing loved ones.

"Elizabeth is writing," I told the charge nurse. I could hardly believe it.

"Fantastic," she said calmly. "You'd better not leave her alone for long. We don't have time to clean pencil marks off the walls tonight." She turned away, avoiding my eyes. "Oh, I almost forgot. Novak and Sellers both have that rotten flu. They'll be out all week. Looks like you'll be working Christmas Eve." She pulled a metal-backed chart from the file and was suddenly very busy.

I swallowed hard. Until now I had loved my independence, my own small trailer. At twenty-two, I was just out of nurse's training and on my own. But I had never spent Christmas Eve away from my parents and my brothers. That wasn't in the picture at all when I moved away from home. I planned to go home for the holidays.

Words raced through my head: *They'll go to the candlelight service without me! They'll read the stories, and I won't be there to hear! What kind of Christmas can I have in a little trailer with nothing to decorate but a potted fern? How can it be Christmas if I can't be the first one up to turn on the tree lights? Who'll make the cocoa for the family?*

Tears burned my eyes, but I blinked them back. Nodding slowly, I walked toward the dayroom.

Elizabeth sat at the writing table staring down at the paper in front of her. Softly I touched my hand to her fragile shoulder, and she looked up with a smile. She handed me the paper. Under my big, bold writing was a wobbly signature.

ELIZABETH GOODE it read.

"Doop doop," said Elizabeth with satisfaction.

Later that night, when all the visitors were gone and the north wing was dark and silent, I sat with the charge nurse, completing charts. "Do you suppose I could take Elizabeth out tomorrow?" I asked. In good weather, we often took the patients for walks or rides, but I didn't know about snowy nights. "I'd like to go to the Christmas Eve service, and I think she'd like to go with me."

"Wouldn't she be a problem? What about the *doop doop*?"

"I think I can explain it to her. You know, nobody else talks during church, so she'd probably be quiet too. Look how well she did this afternoon when I gave her something to do."

The charge nurse looked thoughtful. "Things *would* be a lot easier around here if you did take her. Then you could get her ready for bed when you got back. There'll be visitors to help with the others, but nobody has been here for Elizabeth in a long time. I'll ask her doctor for you."

And so it was that a first-year nurse and a tall, skinny old lady arrived at First Church on Christmas Eve just before the service began. The snow had stopped and the stars were brilliant in the clear, cold sky.

"Now, Elizabeth," I said, "I don't know how much you can understand, but listen to me. We're going in to sit down with the rest of the people. There'll be music and someone will read. There'll be kids in costumes too. But we aren't going to say anything. We'll stand up when it's time to sing, and we'll hold the hymnal together."

Elizabeth looked grave. "Doop doop," she said.

Oh, Lord, I hope she understands! I thought. *Suppose she gets up and heads down the aisle wishing everyone a doop doop?*

I wrapped Elizabeth's coat and shawl around her and tucked my arm under hers. Together we entered the candlelit church. Elizabeth's watery old eyes gleamed, and her face crinkled in a smile. But she said nothing.

The choir entered singing. The pastor read the Christmas story from the Bible: "And there were in the same country, shepherds . . ."

Costumed children took their places at the front of the church—shepherds and wise men, angels and the holy family. Elizabeth watched, but she said nothing. The congregation rose to sing "Joy to the World." Elizabeth stood, holding the hymnal with me, her mouth closed. The lights in the sanctuary dimmed, and two white-robed angels lit the candelabra. Finally the organ began the introduction to "Silent Night," and we stood again.

I handed the hymnal to Elizabeth, but she shook her head.

A cold dread gathered at the back of my neck. Now what? Would this be the moment when she started wandering down the aisle? I looked at her wrinkled face out of the corner of my eye, trying to guess her thoughts. The singing began. I sang as loudly as I could, hoping to attract Elizabeth's attention. As I paused for breath, I heard a thin, cracked voice.

"Sleep in heavenly peace," it sang. "Sleep in heavenly peace."

Elizabeth! Staring straight ahead, candlelight reflected in her eyes, she was singing the words without consulting the hymnal.

Oh, Lord, forgive me, I prayed. *Sometimes I forget. Of course it can be Christmas with only a fern to decorate. Of course it can be Christmas without a tree or the family or cocoa. Christmas is the story of love. It's the birth of the Son of God, and it can live in the heart and memory of a gray-haired old woman.*

"Christ the Savior is born," sang Elizabeth. "Christ the Savior is born."

"Merry Christmas, Elizabeth," I whispered, gently patting her arm.

"Doop doop," Elizabeth replied contentedly.

Robin Cole

Robin Cole lives in Verdale, Washington. This article was originally published by Guideposts, *December 1995.*

CHAPTER 12

The Last Christmas

BABBIE MASON

*M*ost people who are familiar with the great reformer Martin Luther see him as a stern figure who had little time for holidays or, for that matter, celebrations of any sort. Yet, did you know that he is credited with originating one of our most cherished traditions—the Christmas tree?

He also beautifully expressed the essence of Christmas when he wrote, centuries ago,

> *There are some of us who think to ourselves, "If I had only been there! How quick I would have been to help the Baby. I would have washed His linen. How happy I would have been to go with the shepherds to see the Lord lying in the*

manger!" . . . We say that because we know how great
Christ is, but if we had been there at that time, we would
have done no better than the people of Bethlehem. Why
don't we do it now? We have Christ in our neighbor.

My own father was a man much like Martin Luther. He was courageous and wise and deeply committed to his faith, his family, and his community. He brought his keen spiritual insight to every endeavor he undertook—whether it was his role as county commissioner, president of the NAACP, host of a live radio broadcast, or professor at a local college—and he boldly stood up for his convictions. Yet he was also a loving father, husband, and pastor who was both my hero and my mentor.

As far back as I can remember, our entire family life revolved around the Lily Baptist Church in Jackson, Michigan, the church my dad founded and served as pastor for forty years. During those eventful decades, I saw my father put his faith into practice countless times. I witnessed his dedication to serving others, and I truly believe, had he been in Bethlehem two thousand years ago, he would have been "quick" to help the Baby; "to go with the shepherds to see the Lord lying in the manger."

You see, I know this because Dad and I were especially close. For many years I served with and worked alongside him in his ministry, both on Sunday morning and throughout the week. Together we would visit an elderly widow who was homebound and unable to regularly attend services; we would pray with a family caught in the grip of domestic turmoil; we would deliver a meal to a bedridden parishioner too sick to stand over a hot stove. For sixteen years I also served as the church pianist (at first only playing in one key!).

After I had moved away from home, Christmas was the one holiday that always reunited us, and a big part of those reunions took place at church. But of all our gatherings, the year that stands out from the others was December 1986, the last Christmas we were all together. Our whole family was there—Mom, Dad, my three brothers, my sisters from Detroit, and the grandchildren. At that time, we had no idea we were celebrating Dad's last Christmas—that three months later he would die of a heart attack.

As always, our day began with a sunrise community church service. By mid-morning, my sister and I were sitting around the family's kitchen table, dicing celery, onions, and peppers under the ever-watchful eye of our mom. As always, she fixed everything from soul food to leg of lamb. Dinner was served in the dining room on our best china, and Dad sat at the head of the table to bless the food, his rich voice filling the room.

"Our most gracious Lord, our hearts are bursting with the good news of great joy that has come to us in the person of Your Son, Jesus Christ. We praise You for the abundance you have brought into our lives and thank You for each person sitting at this table. May the message of Christmas fill our hearts today and throughout the coming year. In the name of Jesus we pray. Amen."

After enjoying the bounty of Mom's table, we all went into the big family room, where Dad dozed in his favorite rocking chair and the guys "coached" the football games on television. We all felt as though we were kids again.

The next year was very different and very difficult. Despite my dad's death, our family decided to gather at our parents' home and celebrate as we always had. Some traditions deserve to be maintained, no matter how the circumstances in our lives change.

My father's life was one of love and service. When I think of him now, another observation Martin Luther made seems appropriate: "Faith, like light, should always be simple and unbending; while love, like warmth, should beam forth on every side, and bend to every necessity of our brethren."

As time has passed, each Christmas becomes a little easier than the last. Our family makes a real effort to get together then. In fact, we make more of an effort today because we realize it's impossible to know what the new year might hold. We look on the holidays with joy and anticipation, although there's an empty spot in our hearts and a face missing at the head of the table. We know our loss is heaven's gain. And we know that "His love, like warmth, continues to beam forth."

Babbie Mason

Babbie Mason is an award-winning gospel songwriter and vocalist, having written countless chart-topping songs for herself and other well-known Christian artists, including "All Rise," "Each One

Reach One," and "God Has Another Plan." Her eleventh and latest project, Heritage of Faith, challenges the believer to embrace the priorities of the Christian faith and pass it on to those they love. Although her music ministry enables her to travel extensively throughout the U.S. and worldwide, Babbie is actively involved in her own community in Atlanta. She regularly visits youth detention centers, women's jails, and teenage crisis pregnancy centers. She and her husband, Charles, have two sons: Jerry and Chaz. This article was originally published in Today's Christian Woman, November/December 1992.

CHAPTER 13

The
Christmas Miracle

MARIE CHAPIAN

It looked bleak. Very little money, barely a roof over our heads, and the weather at 20 degrees below zero. My husband had walked out after ten years of marriage, the children and I were bewildered and frightened, and it was Christmastime.

Our story begins in a Minnesota blizzard. It's 10 P.M. and the kids and I are sitting in Shakey's Pizza off Highway 10. The barely eaten pizza lies cold on the plates before us. We have been sitting silently, staring ahead of us at the empty restaurant. The children are restless. They sense something terrible has happened. I fidget with a napkin, fighting tears. At last, I help my girls into their warm winter coats and woolen hats, I slip on their mittens, I sing a little song. But I'm crying.

"Why did he leave us?" my little girl asks, her eyes wide. "Why did Daddy leave us here like this? How will we get home?"

The restaurant manager clicks the Christmas lights off. In the dark, the hanging strands of fake green boughs take on the look of towels on a clothesline. My husband had driven us here to eat and talk about the children's Christmas. It was supposed to have been a pleasant experience. That's what I had prayed for. I had prayed he would reconsider and come back to his little family. But it had just been a couple of weeks and he was already living with another woman.

I hug my children, explain we're having an adventure. I telephone our church and a colleague from the Christian school where I assistant teach answers. "Do you have snow tires?" I ask, watching the raging storm out the window. The friend on the other end of the phone happened to have a hilarious and outrageous sense of humor. He thought the situation was actually funny.

He arrives in a rattling and clanking old pickup truck minutes later as a scowling restaurant manager locks up. My friend lifts my children into the cab of the pickup.

"What a great guy that husband of yours is: leaves his wife and kids stranded out in the worst storm of the year!"

"Stranded," I repeat.

My friend insists on keeping a sense of humor. "Listen, is God mad at you for something? How'd you get yourself in a situation like this?"

"I believe in miracles. I believe God will answer my prayers," I answer.

My friend is laughing and thumping the palm of his hand on the steering wheel. Soon he's telling jokes and the children lose their worried faces. "How many preachers does it take to change a lightbulb?" The children are giggling.

"Takes two: one to hold the bulb and one to turn the house around." He's laughing and winking at the kids.

I chuckle in spite of myself. "Silly. You made that up."

Then he's telling me about the epic play he plans to write. "Act One will start a million years before the creation of the world." He sniffs back laughter.

"What?"

"You heard right. And Act Two will begin twenty minutes later."

Now *I'm* laughing out loud. On the other side of the window is a wall of white. The storm spreads its fury across the highway and the truck is rocking back and forth in the wind. We shiver. Even with the heater on, our toes are numb with cold.

There are no other cars out on this snowy night. Minnesota people understand bad weather. They don't tempt it. We begin singing choruses the children know.

I love Him better every D-A-Y . . .

A lot of years have passed since that freezing night, looping along the freeway in my friend's rickety old pickup. My beautiful daughters singing "*Jesus loves the little children, all the children of the world*" next to my cheek, me laughing as though it was an ordinary evening, driving home to our real house. But the world seemed to have flopped on its side for me. The bright happiness had left when I became an abandoned wife. The sun went out;

maybe forever, I thought. Still, oddly enough, I could laugh and I could sing.

We didn't get the miracle I prayed for—a reunited family—but we received other miracles, some difficult to explain. What had looked to be a nightmare season of pain, loss, and loneliness became, unequivocally, an exquisite and lovely Christmas.

Imagine. . . . It's about a week until Christmas and the children and I are sitting on the living room floor of our rented apartment, about five miles from the house we had lived in as a two-parent family. We have very little furniture, a few dishes, not much food. I'm thinner than I've ever been. We're singing Christmas carols and drawing pictures with crayons on paper grocery bags.

I decide to be a happy mom. I decide I will not mope around with a droopy countenance. I will teach myself to be happy. My children will have a happy home. No child deserves to live in a house of tears or sorrow. I *believe* with all my heart children deserve the right to be shown the path of joy, and joy isn't always the result of agreeable circumstances. Jesus freely offers us His joy, and I don't want to wait until things are going well to receive it.

Instead, we become a family of singers. We're singing at breakfast. We're singing at lunch, dinner, at night, in bed. *Some trust in chariots and some in horses, but we will remember the name of the Lord our God.*

At night when the children are asleep and I am alone, free to cry, I open my mouth but the words come out in song: *God is so good, God is so good, He's so good to me.* I'm stunned at the power of the Holy Spirit to lift me above our circumstances; I'm amazed at the love I feel. I even begin to refer to myself as a "loved person."

Christmas is close and I have absolutely no money for presents for the children. They attend Christian school, part of which I pay for by assistant teaching. We eat mostly pasta and vegetables that I'm able to buy wholesale by working a few hours each week at a farmer's co-op.

One day, while taking out the garbage, I find an old plastic Christmas tree. Spindly, leaning to one side, only about a foot high, it's green and looks vaguely Christmasy. But, to me, it's beautiful! I rush upstairs to our apartment, announcing that we have our tree. And it's a tree with experience. After disinfecting it in the bathtub, we have a family meeting to discuss the best way to decorate it. We decide to string popcorn.

Great idea. I buy the popcorn and pop it the old-fashioned way—in the frying pan. "The house smells like Christmas," says my little girl. We make papier-mâché angels; we cut out their robes and wings from a silky old bathrobe of mine.

We begin to string the popcorn. We're hungry. We start nibbling. By the end of the evening we've eaten all of it. We're laughing. It's the first time we had heard of anyone eating all the Christmas decorations before they made it to the tree.

We make our Christmas cards—drawing, cutting, and pasting little poems, prayers, and pictures on paper and delivering them to our friends and family. We take part in the many Christmas programs at church, and we wear our best dresses to the beautiful candlelight Christmas Eve service.

When I feel the flood of sadness or loneliness come rushing toward me, I sing. The children sing with me. Their voices are like kisses from God: *Jesus, sweet Jesus, what a wonder You are.*

For the children's presents I find two wooden crate boxes at the supermarket. I merrily carry them home (You'd think I had found gold!) and proceed to turn them into doll cribs. I work at night while the children are asleep. I make two little cloth dolls and sew colorful doll blankets out of scraps. On Christmas Eve, when we return from church, I place them under our scraggly plastic tree, which sits proudly on the table, laden down with happily crayoned paper stars and paper candy canes. Of all the gifts I've given my girls since that first Christmas on our own—trips to Europe, college educations, cars—the gifts they remember as their all-time favorites are those two funny little crate box cribs and the handmade dolls and blankets I placed in them.

But that's not the end of our favorite Christmas story. There is the question of what the children will give to each other and to their mama for Christmas. We talk everyday about God's wonderful gift to us, His Son, Jesus Christ. We read the Christmas story over and over again together. We sing the songs: *Joy to the world, the Lord is come.*

My two girls want to give gifts that are special. *Really* special. God gave His very best for us, after all. So, after making our wrapping paper by painting newspapers in bright tempera colors, each girl lovingly, if not without some hesitation, wraps her favorite toy as a gift to her sister.

And, to my astonishment, the girls greet me with two joyously painted newspaper-wrapped presents on Christmas morning. They have decorated their packages with painted yellow ribbons. I "oooh" and "ahh," admiring their handiwork, which I carefully unwrap. I tell them I'm going to hang these works of art on the wall, and later they help me by holding the ends as I tack them up in the living room. My girls have outshone Picasso!

They are grinning in anticipation as I discover they have wrapped two very dearly loved teddy bears along with the words "I Love You Mom" taped to each. They've given me their most prized possessions.

Years have passed, my girls are grown. Sometimes now, when all is quiet, I think of that long-ago night—of a raging blizzard, my friend's old rickety truck, my little girls' cheeks pressed against mine—on our way to a new apartment without a daddy or a husband. The memory is a million miles from the present, and I feel somewhat ambivalent toward that frightening experience now. I feel a lot of forgiveness, too, which paved the way to my ambivalence.

I'll never forget my friend and his old pickup, though I've long since lost touch with him. He showed me that nothing is too dense with misery to find something to laugh about. I remember telling him as we pushed against the rising blizzard, "I believe in miracles. I really do." But I had no idea the depth and multitude of miracles that would transform our lives.

Don't miracles manifest themselves in the darkest shadows? When it seems light will never find its way through a storm of agonies, there appears a golden ray like dawn across the other-

Eighty-One

wise hopelessly bleak landscape. Jesus came to earth so we can sing and laugh, no matter what storm we're up against.

The smell of popcorn popping will always be special to me. Last year someone sent me some beautiful and expensive silver Christmas ornaments. They are very nice and I appreciate them; but the ornaments I treasure with all my heart—the ornaments I hold in my hands and bless each year—are the crayon-colored cutouts of stars and candy canes the children made during that first Christmas on our own.

We will forever celebrate the birth of joy, the beauty of hope, the gift of eternal life in Christ Jesus. It is with an extravagant gratitude I thank the King of kings. I thank Him for the gift of my daughters, who are my best friends. For a dusty old plastic Christmas tree that became a beautiful emblem of love. For the miracle of a courageous new life. But mostly for the memory of two very loved teddy bears sacrificially and tenderly wrapped in painted newspaper.

Marie Chapian

Marie Chapian is known around the world as the author of more than twenty-five books with translations in fourteen languages, including Chinese and Arabic. Since the publication of her first book in 1972, she has received many awards including two Cornerstone Book of the Year awards, the coveted Gold Medallion Book Award, and a Silver Angel award. Educated at

Moody Bible Institute, the University of Minnesota, Metropolitan State University, the University of California at San Diego, and Vermont College, she holds a doctorate in counseling and an MFA in creative writing. Her best-selling books include Telling Yourself the Truth, Mothers and Daughters, Free to Be Thin, *and a devotional series,* A Heart for God.

CHAPTER 14

"I Knew You Would Come"

ELIZABETH KING ENGLISH

*H*erman and I locked our store and dragged ourselves home to South Caldwell Street. It was 11:00 P.M., Christmas Eve of 1949. We were dog tired.

Ours was one of those big old general appliance stores that sold everything from refrigerators, toasters, and record players to bicycles, dollhouses, and games. We had sold almost all of our toys; and all of the layaways, except one package, had been picked up.

Usually Herman and I kept the store open until everything had been claimed. We couldn't have woken up happy on Christmas morning, knowing that some child's gift was still on the layaway shelf. But the person who had put a dollar down on that package never returned.

Early Christmas morning our twelve-year-old son, Tom, and Herman and I were by the tree opening gifts. But I'll tell you, there was something humdrum about this Christmas. Tom was growing up, he had wanted just clothes and games. I missed his childish exuberance of past years.

As soon as breakfast was over Tom left to visit his friend next door. Herman mumbled, "I'm going back to sleep. There's nothing left to stay up for."

So there I was alone, doing the dishes and feeling let down. It was nearly 9:00 A.M., and sleet mixed with snow cut the air outside. The wind rattled our windows, and I felt grateful for the warmth of the apartment. *Sure glad I don't have to go out on a day like today,* I thought, picking up the wrapping paper and ribbons strewn around the living room.

And then it began. Something I had never experienced before. A strange, persistent urge. It seemed to be telling me to go to the store.

I looked at the icy sidewalk outside. *That's crazy,* I said to myself. I tried dismissing the urge, but it wouldn't leave me alone. In fact, it was getting stronger.

Well, I *wasn't* going to go. I had never gone to the store on Christmas Day in all the ten years we had owned it. No one opened shops on that day. There wasn't any reason to go, I didn't want to, and I wasn't going to.

For an hour I fought that strange feeling. Finally, I couldn't stand it any longer, and I got dressed.

"Herman," I said, feeling silly, "I think I'll walk down to the store."

Herman woke with a start. "Whatever for? What are you going to do there?"

"Oh, I don't know," I replied lamely. "There's not much to do here. I think I'll just wander down."

He argued against it a little, but I told him that I would be back soon. "Well, go on," he grumped, "but I don't see any reason for it."

I put on my gray wool coat, then my galoshes, red scarf, and gloves. Once outside, none of those garments seemed to help. The wind cut right through me and the sleet stung my cheeks. I groped my way the mile down to 117 East Park Avenue, slipping and sliding.

I shivered and tucked my hands inside my pockets to keep them from freezing. I felt ridiculous. I had no business being out in the bitter chill.

There was the store just ahead. In front of it stood two boys, one about nine and the other six. *What in the world?* I wondered.

"Here she comes!" yelled the older one. He had his arm around the younger. "See, I told you she would come," he said jubilantly.

They were black children, and they were half frozen. The younger one's face was wet with tears, but when he saw me, his eyes opened wide and his sobbing stopped.

"What are you two children doing out here in this freezing rain?" I scolded, hurrying them into the store and turning up the heat. "You should be at home on a day like this!" They were poorly dressed. They had no hats or gloves, and their shoes barely held together. I rubbed their small icy hands, and got them up close to the heater.

"We've been waiting for you," replied the older boy. He told me they had been standing outside since 9:00 A.M., the time I normally opened the store.

"Why were you waiting for me?" I asked, astonished.

"My little brother Jimmy didn't get any Christmas." He touched Jimmy's shoulder. "We want to buy some skates. That's what he wants. We have these three dollars. See, Miss Lady?" he said, pulling the bills from his pocket.

I looked at the money in his hand. I looked at their expectant faces. And then I looked around the store. "I'm sorry," I said, "but we've sold almost everything. We have no—" Then my eyes caught sight of the layaway shelf with its lone package.

"Wait a minute," I told the boys. I walked over, picked up the package, unwrapped it and, miracle of miracles, there was a pair of skates!

Jimmy reached for them. *Lord*, I prayed silently, *let them be his size.*

And miracle added upon miracle, they *were* his size.

When the older boy finished tying the laces on Jimmy's right skate and saw that it fit—perfectly—he stood up and presented the dollars to me.

"No, I'm not going to take your money," I told him. I *couldn't* take his money. "I want you to have these skates, and I want you to use your money to get some gloves."

The boys just blinked at first. Then their eyes became like

saucers, and their grins stretched wide when they understood I was giving them the skates.

What I saw in Jimmy's eyes was like a blessing. It was pure joy, and it was beautiful. My spirits rose.

After the children had warmed up, I turned down the heater, and we walked out together. As I locked the door, I turned to the older brother and said, "How lucky that I happened to come along when I did. If you had stood there much longer, you would have frozen. But how did you boys know I would come?"

I wasn't prepared for his reply. His gaze was steady, and he answered me softly, "I knew you would come," he said. "I asked Jesus to send you."

The tingles in my spine weren't from the cold, I knew. God had planned this.

As we waved good-bye, I turned home to a brighter Christmas than I had left. Tom brought his friend over to our house. Herman got out of bed; his father, "Papa" English, and sister Ella came by. We had a delicious dinner and a wonderful time.

But the one thing that made the Christmas really joyous was the one thing that makes every Christmas wonderful: Jesus was there.

Elizabeth English

Elizabeth English lives in Charlotte, North Carolina. This article was originally published in Guideposts, *December 1995.*

CHAPTER 15

Alone at the Manger

MICHELLE VAN LOON

$\mathcal{G}$rowing up Jewish, I never gave Christmas more than a fleeting thought. It was the other December holiday. When I saw dazzling toy advertisements on television, I simply substituted the word *Chanukah* for *Christmas*. Christmas vacation from school was merely a subtle reminder that there were many more Gentiles in the world than Jews.

But when I was thirteen, my family moved into a non-Jewish area. It was a difficult adjustment for us. Though my parents were not especially religious, they taught us to love Jewish culture and life. My heritage, which once had defined me, now set me apart from my peers. My Jewishness met with reactions ranging from good-natured teasing to full-blown anti-Semitism.

The one thing that most thirteen-year-olds want more than anything else is to be like everyone else. Being different flooded my heart with questions. Where did I fit in? Why was my religion so important? Who was God anyway?

A year went by. I still struggled to fit in. One day, over the din in the cafeteria, a classmate announced that she had become a Christian. "I thought you were a Christian," I said. "Aren't all non-Jews Christians?"

Karen shook her head. "Everyone needs forgiveness. Jesus died for my sins, and for yours too. He loves you!" Her joyful words poured salt into my lonely, wounded heart.

I sorted through my Old Testament, trying to understand what being Jewish meant. But I couldn't escape what Karen was telling me about Jesus. My parents had always told me He was a great teacher, but not *our* teacher. Karen said He was more than a teacher. He was the Son of God, the Messiah, and Savior.

The question of who Jesus was alternately attracted and terrified me. I was intrigued by the boldness of His claims. Yet my parents angrily dismissed my inquiries. "Jesus is *their* God," they said. "Jews have nothing to do with Him."

Their answer left me unsatisfied. For months, I pelted Karen with questions: "Why did Jesus have to die?" "How could His mom be a virgin?" "I was always taught that God is one. Explain the Trinity." My friend, a brand-new Christian, certainly was no theologian. But she demonstrated patience, love, and a changed life that went beyond simple answers.

Finally, Karen suggested that I talk with an older friend. He listened to my questions and tried to answer them from Scripture. His final words exposed my heart, which had been teetering on the brink of belief. "I think you're hiding behind all of these questions," he said softly. "God is asking you to make a decision. What are you going to do about Jesus?"

Unable to look him in the eye, I ended the conversation abruptly. I was painfully aware of my distance from God. King David's cry became mine: "For I acknowledge my transgressions, and my sin is always before me" (Ps. 51:3).

I finally gathered the courage to read the New Testament, beginning with the gospel of John. "Lord, I want to know who this Jesus really is," I prayed. I soon came to John 14:6: "I am the way, the truth, and the life. No one comes to the Father except through Me."

Though I still had many questions, I understood that Jesus alone could bring me into a relationship with God. I realized that He had died for me, to pay the penalty for my sins. And I believed that He had risen from the dead. In prayer, I committed myself to Him.

It was many months before I told my parents. I had heard stories of other Jewish parents calling in cult deprogrammers or disowning children who believed in Jesus. Because my parents prided themselves on their open-mindedness, I didn't expect anything that extreme. But I knew that they would see my new faith as a slap in the face.

I longed to go to church. Even more, I wanted them to know the good news that Jesus was their Messiah. So I told them what had happened to me, knowing there was no turning back.

"Michelle, you can't expect us to be happy about this conversion of yours," my mother said grimly. "We will never approve."

My dad's eyes were deep pools of hurt and anger. He spit each word. "I do not want to hear about your new religion. Ever. And you will never be allowed to attend church as long as you live under my roof."

Jesus' words spoke directly to my situation. "I did not come to bring peace but a sword," He said. "For I have come to 'set a man against his father, a daughter against her mother, a daughter-in-law against her mother-in-law'; and 'a man's enemies will be those of his own household'" (Matt. 10:34–36).

I sensed the depths of God's love for me during that time. I was hungry to know Him better, and my hunger drew me to several sources of spiritual food: books, fellowship with other Christians at school, and the local Christian radio station.

As my first Christmas as a believer approached, I suddenly awoke to the holiday I had long ignored. Images of happy family gatherings, of youth group caroling parties, of solemn Christmas Eve candlelight services, and mountains of gifts under a fragrant tinseled tree all came into focus for the first time in my life. I wanted to participate somehow.

I approached my parents gingerly. "Do you think I could go to church with Karen on Christmas Eve, just this once?"

"Isn't our holiday good enough for you?" my mom responded.

"Christmas is different. All I want is the chance to visit—"

"Absolutely not." My dad, normally a jovial man, ended the conversation harshly. I walked out of the room, disappointed. I could hear them reassuring each other that my newfound faith was surely just a fad.

The tension inside me mounted as Christmas approached. Everywhere I went, it seemed that people were busily preparing for December 25. Just a short time earlier in my life, I couldn't have even pinpointed the date for Christmas. Now, I longed to experience it. *In a few more years*, I told myself, *I'll be able to celebrate Christmas like everyone else*.

When Christmas Eve finally came, I went into my room and tuned my radio to some Christmas carols. I heard them as if for the first time, not as Muzak in a mall, but as breathtaking praise. I spent the evening with God's Word, alone but not lonely. I woke Christmas morning, not to a house filled with laughter and presents, but with a sense of awe for God's gift of His Son . . . for me!

* * *

Karen, the friend who pointed the way to Jesus, stood in the kitchen the day after Christmas in 1992, nearly two decades since that first solitary Christmas. We were reminiscing, our conversation punctuated by the happy clatter of our children.

"It seems like only yesterday," she began, then we both laughed.

"I spent so much time dreaming of Christmases like these back when we were in high school," I remarked. "But now that I have the ability to celebrate however I choose, I'm content to celebrate simply."

As a new Christian, I could never have pictured the pressure that often accompanies the frenzied holiday activity. There are programs to attend, people to shop for, guests to entertain, cookies to bake, trees to decorate. The money-and-time crunch, all in the name of Christmas, conspires to rob the season of its joy. For more families than I ever dreamed, the season is packed with tension and unfulfilled expectations.

But for me, those years of celebrating alone in my room stripped the holiday of all but the baby King resting in the feeding trough. I continue to be in awe of what Jesus' birthday meant in God's eternal plan: "Who, being in the form of God, did not consider it robbery to be equal with God, but made Himself of no reputation, taking the form of a bondservant, and coming in the likeness of men" (Phil. 2:6, 7).

I've learned there is only one thing necessary to celebrate Christmas properly: Jesus Christ.

Michelle Van Loon

Michelle Van Loon is a homemaker and freelance writer in Waukesha, Wisconsin. Her husband, Bill, and she have two sons, Ben and Jacob, and a daughter, Rachel. Michele recently became a foster parent with Bethany Christian Services. This article was originally published in Moody, *December 1993.*

CHAPTER 16

Marty's Secret

DIANE RAYNER

$\mathscr{T}$ grew up believing that Christmas was a time when strange and wonderful things happened, when wise and royal visitors came riding, when at midnight the barnyard animals talked to one another, and in the light of a fabulous star God came down to us as a child. Christmas to me has always been a time of enchantment, and never more so than the year my son Marty was eight.

That was the year my children and I moved into a cozy trailer home in a forested area just outside of Redmond, Washington. As the holiday approached, our spirits were lightened, not to be dampened even by the winter rains that swept down Puget Sound to douse our home and make our floors muddy.

Throughout that December, Marty had been the most spirited and busiest of us all. He was my youngest, a cheerful boy, blond and playful, with a quaint habit of looking up at you and cocking his head like a puppy when you spoke to him. The reason for this was that Marty was deaf in his left ear, but it was a condition he never complained about.

For weeks I had been watching Marty. I knew something was going on that he was not telling me about. I saw how eagerly he made his bed, took out the trash, and carefully set the table and helped Rick and Pam prepare dinner before I got home from work. I saw how he silently collected his allowance and tucked it away, not spending a cent of it. I had no idea what all this quiet activity was about, but I suspected it had something to do with Kenny.

Kenny was Marty's friend, and ever since they had found each other in the springtime, they were seldom apart. If you called to one, you got them both. Their world was in the meadow—a horse pasture broken by a small winding stream— where they caught frogs and snakes, searched for arrowheads and hidden treasure, or spent afternoons feeding peanuts to squirrels.

Times were hard for our family, and we had to do some scrimping to get by. Thanks to my job as a meat wrapper and a lot of ingenuity, we managed to have elegance on a shoestring. But not Kenny's family. They were desperately poor, and his mother was struggling to feed and clothe her two children. They were a good, solid family; but Kenny's mom was a proud woman, and she had strict rules.

How we worked, as we did each year, to make our home festive for the holiday! Ours was a handcrafted Christmas of gifts hidden away and ornaments strung about the place.

Marty and Kenny sometimes sat still at the table long enough to help make cornucopias or weave baskets for the tree; but then one whispered to the other, and they were out the door in a flash, and sliding cautiously under the electric fence into the horse pasture that separated our home from Kenny's.

One night shortly before Christmas, when my hands were deep in *peppernoder* dough, shaping nutlike Danish cookies heavily spiced with cinnamon, Marty came to me and said in a tone mixed with pleasure and pride, "Mom, I've bought Kenny a Christmas present. Want to see it?"

So that's what he's been up to, I thought.

"It's something he's wanted for a long, long time, Mom."

After carefully wiping his hands on a dish towel, he pulled a small box from his pocket. Lifting the lid, I gazed at the pocket compass that my son had been saving all those allowances to buy.

"It's a lovely gift, Martin," I said, but even as I spoke, a disturbing thought came to mind. I knew how Kenny's mother felt about their poverty. They could barely afford to exchange gifts among themselves, and giving presents to others was out of the question. I was sure she would not permit her son to receive something he could not return in kind.

Gently, carefully, I talked over the problem with Marty. He understood what I was saying.

"I know, Mom, I know . . . but what if it was a *secret*? What if they never found out *who* gave it?"

I didn't know how to answer him.

The day before Christmas was rainy, cold, and gray. The three kids and I all but fell over one another as we elbowed our way about our home putting finishing touches on secret Christmas gifts and preparing for family and friends who would drop by.

Night settled in. The rain continued. I looked out the window over the sink and felt an odd sadness. How mundane the rain seemed for a Christmas Eve. Would wise men come on such a night? I doubted it. It seemed to me that strange and wonderful things happened only on clear nights, nights when one could at least see a star in the heavens.

I turned from the window, and as I checked on the ham and *lefse* bread warming in the oven, I saw Marty slip out the door. He wore his coat over his pajamas, and he clutched a tiny, colorfully wrapped box.

Down through the soggy pasture he went, then under the electric fence and across the yard to Kenny's house. Up the steps on tiptoe, shoes squishing; open the screen door just a crack; place the gift on the doorstep; then take a deep breath, reach for the doorbell and press on it *hard*.

Quickly Marty turned and ran down the steps and across the yard in a wild race to get away unnoticed. Then, suddenly, he banged into the electric fence.

The shock sent him reeling. He lay stunned on the wet ground. His body tingled and he gasped for breath. Then slowly, weakly, confused and frightened, he began the grueling trip back home.

"Marty," I cried as he stumbled through the door, "what happened?" His lower lip quivered, his eyes brimmed.

"I forgot about the fence, and it knocked me down!"

I hugged his muddy body to me. He was still dazed, and there was a red mark beginning to blister on his face from his mouth to his ear. Quickly I treated the blister and, with a warm cup of cocoa soothing him, Marty's bright spirits returned. I tucked him into bed and just before he fell asleep he looked up at me and said, "Mom, Kenny didn't see me. I'm sure he didn't see me."

That Christmas Eve I went to bed unhappy and puzzled. It seemed such a cruel thing to happen to a little boy who was doing what the Lord wants us all to do, giving to others, and giving in secret at that. I did not sleep well that night. Somewhere deep inside I must have been feeling the disappointment that Christmas had come and it had been just an ordinary, problem-filled night, no mysterious enchantment at all.

But I was wrong. By morning the rain stopped and the sun shone. The streak on Marty's face was red, but I could tell that the burn was not serious. We opened our presents, and soon, not unexpectedly, Kenny was knocking on the door, eager to show Marty his new compass and tell about the mystery of its arrival. It was plain that Kenny didn't suspect Marty at all, and while the two of them talked, Marty just smiled and smiled.

Then I noticed that while the two boys were comparing their Christmases, nodding and gesturing and chattering away, Marty was not cocking his head when Kenny was talking. Marty seemed to be listening with his deaf ear. Weeks later a report came from the school nurse, verifying what Marty and I already knew: "Marty now has complete hearing in both ears."

How Marty regained his hearing, and still has it, remains a mystery. Doctors suspect that the shock from the electric fence was somehow responsible. Perhaps so. Whatever the reason, I am thankful to God for the good exchange of gifts that was made that night.

So you see, strange and wonderful things still happen on the night of our Lord's birth. And one does not have to have a clear night, either, to follow a fabulous star.

Diane Rayner

Diane Rayner is a freelance writer from Freeland, Washington. This article was originally published in Guideposts, *December 1995.*

CHAPTER 17

Our First Christmas

SHIRLEY BOONE

$\mathcal{I}$t was our second Christmas together as a young married couple, but our first alone, completely on our own in Denton, Texas. We were married at nineteen, so our first Christmas had been spent in Nashville, both with my family and with Pat's. It was wonderful.

But then we moved to Denton where Pat was enrolled at North Texas State University as a sophomore. We were just two young kids with no money and few friends. We were living in a little three-room upstairs student apartment. All we had, literally, was each other. It was going to be a decidedly different kind of holiday from any we'd ever known. Somehow, though, it turned out to be the most moving and, in many ways, the best Christmas we have shared together.

Since we had no money to spend, we both had to become very creative. Somewhere we found a little piece of fir, put it on a stand, and stood it on top of a cardboard box in our tiny front room. We covered the box with cotton snow and found a few decorations people had thrown out that we put on the "tree." We thought we were all set until one of us remembered: What about presents?

I knew Pat had recently done a concert with the Texas Boys Choir in Ft. Worth and that someone had recorded his solo. I arranged for an acetate recording of the entire performance, wrapped it, and put it under the tree. Christmas morning he was absolutely delighted with his keepsake present. In fact, he still has it!

On Christmas Eve Pat placed a big box gaily wrapped in borrowed Christmas paper under the tree for me. I wondered how in the world he had managed to get me anything this big, considering our financial condition. I carefully opened the package, only to discover another smaller package inside. I opened that one and, you guessed it, found an even smaller one.

Finally, after the room seemed filled with boxes and paper, I came to the gift. It was a handmade card that said "I Love You" in large letters.

I know it sounds hokey and sentimental, but that Christmas we gave each other the gift of ourselves. And what we enjoyed was a special sense of the presence and beauty of the One who started the whole Christmas tradition—by giving us Himself.

Shirley Boone

Shirley Boone was born in Chicago, Illinois, the daughter of country music performers Eva and Red Foley. As a very young child she sang occasionally with her parents on radio station WLS in Chicago. In 1953, while still in her teens, she met the man who would soon become her husband, singer Pat Boone. She jokingly says that she has spent her life being Red Foley's daughter, Pat Boone's wife, and the Boone girls' mother. Shirley has served with her family as National Entertainment Chairmen for the March of Dimes, was honorary California Mother of the Year in the early 1970s, and published a book entitled One Woman's Liberation.

CHAPTER 18

"Baby Jesus Is Broken"

BARBARA J. HAMPTON

*M*om, baby Jesus is broken," Karen, my eight-year-old, said. I groaned. The accident could easily become the straw that broke the camel's back. And not the camel in the nativity scene, either. My husband was in the hospital recovering from surgery. I had to make a dozen phone calls concerning the next day's Sunday school Christmas program. Would the rehearsal of the third- and fourth-graders this afternoon at my house be enough to stabilize it, or should I substitute something easier? The pressures were converging when baby Jesus crashed to the floor.

I needed no imagination to guess which baby Jesus had broken. It was the brightly painted terra-cotta baby Jesus, boldly and proudly African, that the girls' Aunt Robin, a missionary nurse in the Ivory Coast, had given to us. It was my most treasured crèche.

The night before we had arranged it on the mantel, twining pine boughs among the pieces. My warnings were so stern that careful Jenny decided just to sit by and watch Ellen, Karen, and me.

I hadn't, however, told Karen not to play with it. How could I have forgotten that she needed that specific instruction? It was my own fault, really. Now she was hovering beside me with her usual apology: "I didn't mean to do it. It was just an accident." As if that would put the figure together again and make everything right.

I dried my hands and went to inspect the damage. Baby Jesus lay in three pieces on the floor. I picked them up and laid them back in the packing-straw manger. Jesus' African mother and Joseph, the shepherds, the wise men, and the women bearing loads on their heads all continued their watch over him, unperturbed. I didn't have time to repair Him then; the day's tasks were pressing too urgently. But throughout the day I mourned the broken figurine.

I loved my crèches. They reminded me each year of the particularity of the Incarnation. God became man, one certain man; but each culture that has accepted that wondrous truth has claimed Jesus as its own. For Africans the baby looks African; for the Japanese, Japanese; and for those of us with European heritage, He looks European. But we dare not claim Him as ours exclusively.

The African crèche was my favorite, not only because it reminded me of this truth but also because of the difficult year we had lived in Liberia. Karen was born that year. Surrounded as we were by abject poverty, we realized more fully how mean and lowly—how despicable—was Jesus' chosen lot. Karen wasn't born in a stable, but neither was the mission hospital equipped with the comforts that Western medicine can provide. I experienced perhaps a measure of what Mary must have felt when she gave birth far from her home in Nazareth.

Soon after our return to the States, Karen suffered a violent, prolonged seizure, the first of hundreds to come. More than once we almost lost her. Last Christmas—again across the ocean from home—a seizure was followed by pneumonia. For more than three weeks Karen lay in a hospital bed among wires and tubes and monitors, fighting back from a brush with death. Now eight years old and heavily medicated, she was struggling with first-grade work in a learning disabilities class.

Broken. The word echoed in my mind, reminding me of Isaiah 53. It wasn't a typical Advent passage, but didn't it predict the fate of the baby and the purpose for which He was born?

> *He is despised and rejected by men,*
> *A Man of sorrows and acquainted with grief.*
> *And we hid, as it were, our faces from Him;*
> *He was despised, and we did not esteem Him.*
> *Surely He has borne our griefs*
> *And carried our sorrows;*
> *Yet we esteemed Him stricken,*

Smitten by God, and afflicted.
But He was wounded for our transgressions,
He was bruised for our iniquities;
The chastisement for our peace was upon Him,
And by His stripes we are healed.

(Isa. 53:3–5)

Even though Jesus' tiny body was perfect—the sacrificial Lamb had to be without spot or blemish—even though He was loved, adored, and worshiped the night He was born, already He was despised. A King? In a smelly stable? He was just a Jewish nobody in a power-hungry world. In a few short years people would sneer, "Can anything good come out of Nazareth?" Or, "Look how He goes around with prostitutes and tax collectors!" In the end the sin of even those who loved Him the night of His birth and those who would love Him through the centuries would break Him.

Break. The word was too weak. Karen did not know more graphic ones, but Isaiah had not spared them: *stricken, smitten, afflicted, pierced, crushed, despised, rejected.*

Karen, I thought, *you spoke truer than you knew.* The next morning we snuggled in bed together and talked. I told her how baby Jesus had come so that He could be broken on the cross. We broke the real Jesus, she and I and everyone, with our sins. And—I thought of the rest of Isaiah's prophecy—He was broken so that her own physical and mental brokenness could be made whole.

I tried to keep my words simple. Jesus loved her and would

give her to His Father someday, perfect and whole. She wouldn't have seizures anymore. She wouldn't get pneumonia. No one would laugh at her and make her cry. What was her part? She would have to be sorry for how she had broken Jesus. She would have to love and obey Him.

I stopped. I had used too many words and described abstractions too complex for her to grasp. She already loved baby Jesus in her own way. She loves all babies passionately. This particular baby story, however, is so tangible each Christmas. Perhaps the figure broken in three pieces would be equally tangible and powerful for her, becoming something she could see, touch, and begin to understand. Perhaps it is just as well that glue would not mend the porous clay.

This year, when the five of us put out the African crèche, we will read Isaiah 53. Perhaps Karen will be reading well enough to take her turn. We will let her put the broken baby Jesus in His spot of honor on the mantel. Perhaps she will remember our theological talk, but if not, we will simplify and repeat it. Even if she does not remember, I will. I'll remember what my little girl, broken though she is, taught me the morning she came into the kitchen to confess that "Baby Jesus is broken."

Barbara Hampton

Barbara Hampton is a consultant for the Writing Center of the College of Wooster, Wooster, Ohio, and an adjunct professor for the college's First Year Seminar and English Composition classes. In addition to several published articles, she is the coauthor with Gladys Hunt of Read for Your Life. She and her husband, Charles, have three daughters: Jenny, Ellen, and Karen. This article was originally published in Moody, December 1986.

CHAPTER 19

Frozen Pictures of Christmas

BARBARA JOHNSON

*E*veryone has memories, both good and bad, of Christmases past. Since Christmas is such a joyous, hectic, emotional, year-end frenzy of buying and giving and baking (or ordering takeout!) and mailing and you name it (Whew, I'm tired thinking about it!), our memories are stronger than at any other time of the year. That's why I call them the "frozen pictures" of Christmas; they stay frozen in our minds from one year to the next.

Most Christmas memories, of course, revolve around family. Mine are centered on my four sons: Tim, Steve, David, and Barney.

Tim, our oldest, was killed by a drunk driver when he was twenty-three years old. He is our deposit in heaven now. When he was ten, we started a Christmas tradition of spraying several pounds of unshelled nuts with a gold gilt paint and then mixing them together with homemade cookies. We would spread the nuts out on our porch and then Tim would spray them with the gilt.

One year I failed to check the type of paint he bought. As it turned out, it was a hardware store brand that contained a heavy concentration of lead. Of course, he didn't know this was a problem. To him, all gold paints were created equal. He merrily sprayed all the nuts, and then we mixed them in with the cookies.

Several days after distributing them to our friends we began to receive some odd phone calls. "There are strange smells coming from those cookies you gave us," one friend said. "What are you trying to do, kill me?" another joked. Evidently the fumes from the paint had soaked into the nuts and made them inedible. Believe me, it was a "nutty" Christmas. We were just glad no one had gotten sick from them.

Our son David is the musical one in the family. When he was in the fourth grade, his music teacher chose him to sing a solo for his school's Christmas program. The song was "While Shepherds Watched Their Flocks by Night." In jest, we kidded him about singing different words to the song, like, "While shepherds washed their socks by night, the angel of the Lord came down and said, 'Will you wash mine?'"

We continued to sing these crazy lyrics and teased him about his big night, telling him that he would forget the real words and have to use ours. One day while he was practicing I even jokingly said I would pay him five dollars if he would sing the wrong lyrics. Being a "professional," he, of course, said that no amount of money in the world would make him embarrass himself by doing such a dumb thing.

Well, the big night came, David got up to sing his solo, and—you guessed it!— he opened his mouth and out came, "While shepherds washed their socks by night . . ." After the first line, he realized what he had done. But, rather than correct himself, this smart little guy kept going as if nothing unusual had happened. He was so confident that the audience wasn't sure if he had made a mistake or not. He ended up being the hit of the program, and everyone, including his puzzled music teacher, gave him a rousing ovation.

The baby in our family is Barney. He is also our Christmas baby since he was born in late December. When I brought him home from the hospital on Christmas morning, I put a bright red stocking on his head.

He was such a beautiful baby—the only good-looking one I had. But he also had colic. If anyone reading this has had a colicky child, they will know what I mean when I say that if he had been my first, he would have been the last!

The only way I could get him to sleep was to wrap him snugly in a blanket and set him in a basket on the clothes dryer—*on* it, not *in* it! The vibration of the dryer and the continuous droning would keep him asleep. My problem was that the dryer only ran for sixty minutes before it shut off. I would have to set my alarm clock for fifty-eight minutes past the hour, wearily get out of bed, and turn the dryer on again for another hour so he wouldn't wake up. This worked fine until he was about seven months old and learned to crawl off the dryer. I'm sure Mary never had such problems with *her* "Christmas Baby."

My strongest Christmas memory, though, is the last time our son Steve was home for the holidays. You see, Steve was killed in Vietnam at the age of eighteen. That Christmas he was in marine training camp in San Diego and was close enough to us to come home for the holidays.

Steve brought a young friend with him from camp whose family lived in North Carolina. Because their leave was so short, he couldn't make it home in time and decided to spend the holidays with us. That year everything in the house was perfect for a Christmas celebration. The aroma of cinnamon and popcorn (a family favorite!) wafted throughout our beautifully decorated house. The crisp sounds of laughter, mixed with the crackling log in the fireplace, created a warm holiday atmosphere.

It was a cold, rainy night when they arrived. After discarding their damp jackets, Steve's friend went over to the fireplace to warm himself. His first words were, "Boy, it's so good to be home!" We had supper and both boys ate ravenously. After letting out a deep sigh, Steve's friend again said, "It sure is wonderful to be home!"

We opened our Christmas presents that evening since the boys had to be back the next day. Before he left, Steve's friend once again said, with a huge smile, "Man, it is just so good to have been home for Christmas!" A few weeks later both of these valiant young men were killed during a major battle in Vietnam. They are both now in their heavenly home. Whenever someone says that familiar phrase, "It's so good to be home," I immediately think of that Christmas and the special time we had together as a "family."

Christmas has many frozen pictures for me. Some are poignant, some are bittersweet. But all are vivid in my mind and heart.

Barbara Johnson

Humorist Barbara Johnson is the founder of Spatula Ministries, an organization designed to "peel parents off the ceiling with a spatula of love and begin them on the road to recovery." Barbara's wit has helped her survive devastating experiences. Her husband, Bill, was in a near-fatal accident; she lost one son in Vietnam and another to a drunk driver; and a third son became involved in a homosexual lifestyle. She has learned that although pain is inevitable for everyone, people can "choose to pick flowers instead of weeds." Barbara wrote her first book after the age of fifty, and is the author of such best-selling titles as Where Does a Mother Go to Resign?, Stick a Geranium in Your Hat and Be Happy, *and* Pack Up the Gloomies in a Great Big Box, Then Sit on the Lid and Laugh.

CHAPTER 20

Macaroni Christmas

KAREN L. PROWITZ

*T*oday my husband, Paul, would be labeled a victim of corporate downsizing. In the early 1980s, however, it was simply called being out of work; and it couldn't have happened at a worse time—Christmas. With only enough savings to see us through mid-January, the approaching holidays seemed bleak. Any money found in the Christmas cards we received was quickly spent on overdue bills and necessities.

Our three children, David, Vikki, and Daniel—then ages seven through twelve—were old enough to understand our predicament, yet still at the age when they would miss a festive tree stacked high with brightly wrapped presents. We were proud of them for behaving like good little troopers as Christmas approached, but as parents, we hurt inside knowing their holidays weren't going to be nearly as merry as the one enjoyed by their friends.

I tried to remind myself that the first Christmas found Jesus in a common manger, surrounded by coarse hay, animal smells, and barnyard noises. No glittering tree or expensive gifts had marked His birth. Only the love and joy of Joseph and Mary and the awe of humble shepherds. It was such a simple, stark entry for a newborn King.

Paul and I talked a lot as the days passed about materialism and how easy it is to lose sight of the true meaning of Christmas. I even caught myself becoming a bit smug about the fact that our family was celebrating Christmas without all the usual "secular trappings," as if it were simply a matter of personal choice rather than necessity.

We prayed often during this painful time, and the Lord faithfully gave us the strength we needed. Yet the nagging question remained, "What about the children?" This Christmas was certain to be a disappointment for them, even if they weren't complaining. Could His grace also comfort them?

Then the last school bell before holiday break rang out and the bus door opened on our street to the squeals of happy students. Only three days remained until the big day. We were glad to have the children home, but now the vision of a meager Christmas morning was beginning to loom even bigger. We asked the Lord to help us focus on Him as a family and to keep alive the hope of a new job for Paul.

A small monetary gift had arrived in a card that day, and it was quickly earmarked for holiday baking. We were *not* going to miss the fun of making Christmas cookies! Daniel always entertained us with his unique decorating ideas and unusual frosting color concoctions, including purple Christmas trees. Finishing the last couple of dozen cookies alone, flour everywhere, colored sugar crystals and silver balls crunching under my feet, I truly appreciated this simple, holiday pleasure.

On Christmas Eve most of the day was spent cleaning the house and bringing up the old artificial tree, trimmings, lights, and room decorations from the basement closet. By mid-afternoon, we were ready to bake our annual birthday cake for Jesus. The kids had always felt He would like chocolate cake with vanilla frosting. We had started the tradition of baking a birthday cake for Jesus as a way to focus on the *real* reason we celebrate Christmas. This lesson had seemed much more necessary in previous years when we had taken for granted family trips to the area shopping malls.

After supper, Paul and David put the lights on the tree. The rest of us waited patiently to begin hanging ornaments and arranging the shimmering garlands. Soon the boys tired of the decorating and left Vikki and me to finish up.

Since childhood, creating a village scene and arranging the crèche beneath the tree had been my special job. Now Vikki joined me as we draped folds of white satin around the tree trunk. Magically the cloth became snowdrifts brushing against the sides of tiny cardboard houses. Tall pinecones became a forest behind the village, while chubby, squat cones posed as evergreen trees. An old mirror became a skating pond dusted lightly with artificial snow. A plastic deer stood in the middle of the pond, head lifted high as if listening to a choir within the miniature white steepled church.

Next the crèche was carefully placed into the village scene. The satin cloth was smoothed down so we could place a hand-made needlepoint ornament in front of the crèche. Its white stitches etched a crown and proclaimed in red lettering, "Jesus Christ—King of kings." Vikki and I sat still for a moment to drink in the peaceful serenity of the holy scene.

The time had finally come to put the gifts under the tree—all four of them. My parents had sent a box with gifts for each of the children and a combined gift for Paul and me. There were assorted little items like candy canes and prefilled stockings, but the vast emptiness of the white satin cloth seemed to mock our decorating efforts. It looked pretty grim as Vikki and I cuddled on the couch together.

Suddenly an idea came to me. Paul and the boys had already gone to bed, having prepared themselves for the rather barren scene that would greet them in the morning. But, I decided, they were going to be amazed when they came downstairs. This tree was going to be stacked with presents!

"Vikki! Let's gather all the boxes we can from the kitchen cupboards and wrap them in the leftover Christmas paper from last year. We'll tag each box as a personal gift for one of us. I'll bet we can cover the bottom of this tree with presents!"

"Let's go!" she chimed in.

For the next two hours we wrapped boxes of macaroni and cheese, cereal, cornstarch, rice, pancake mix, powdered sugar, and anything else that came in a box. Each "gift" was marked for Karen, Paul, David, Vikki, or Daniel along with a big, handwritten "Merry Christmas!" tag. When we brought our treasures into the living room, they completely covered the satin cloth under the tree.

Vikki and I went to bed that Christmas Eve, exhausted coconspirators who could hardly wait till morning to see the looks on the boys' faces, not to mention their father's. They would think it was a miracle! Maybe it was.

Daniel was first on the scene. He raced back upstairs to awaken David and Vikki. "Come and see all the presents!" he shouted. Paul slowly rolled over. I could barely contain myself when I saw his confused look. After we had gathered in the living room, David passed out the first round of gifts. Then the fun really began.

"Raisin Bran!?!" David exclaimed with astonishment. Just what every twelve-year-old boy hopes for!

"Cornstarch?" Daniel questioned, eyes big as grapes.

Vikki and I couldn't hold the giggles back any longer as we encouraged them to continue. They quickly caught on to our trick, but played along with us. Each person tried to outdo the others with excitement over their "gifts." Can you imagine a seven-year-old boy gleefully shouting, "Wow! Macaroni! Just what I wanted!"

The four real gifts were almost anticlimactic, though none the less appreciated. Our dog, Randy, barked with as much excitement when we opened our cupboard boxes as when a lovely sweater was held up for display.

Later, when I went into the kitchen to get Jesus' birthday cake, I couldn't help but cherish the peals of laughter coming from the living room. There had been no two-wheel bike, no Barbie Dreamhouse, no boom box; yet the day I had dreaded had become a warm celebration of family joy and love.

I looked at the cake's colorful inscription—"Happy Birthday, Jesus!"—as I slowly lit the candles. "Yes," I whispered, "Happy Birthday, Jesus! And thank *You* for taking a difficult situation and making it something beautiful for our family."

Our children are all in their twenties as we prepare for Christmas 1996. David and Vikki have finished college, and Daniel is working at a nearby retail distribution center. That jobless holiday season now seems very far away. Yet it never fails that, as we gather around the tree, someone will recall with a grin, "Remember our Macaroni Christmas?" And the laughter we cherished begins all over again.

Karen Prowitz

Karen Prowitz and her husband, Paul, live in Oconomowoc, Wisconsin. Karen is employed at Oconomowoc High School as a teaching assistant in an alternative education program. She also is a freelance writer whose work has appeared in Charisma, Today's Christian Woman, Moments with God, *and* The Quiet Hour. *Karen and Paul have been married for almost thirty years and have three grown children.*

CHAPTER 21

A Miracle for Christmas, Please!

CHARLA PEREAU

It was our second Christmas in Guerrero, Mexico, and God had not yet raised up a pastor for the people. Our little church on the orphanage property was filled. Men, women, and children had walked for many miles to meet together and worship the Lord. As the only one who felt the need for a service, I found myself responsible for the program and frightened for four reasons: I was an American, a woman in a man's culture, a person whose public speaking had been limited to Sunday school classes, and I couldn't hurdle the language barrier.

My vast Spanish vocabulary totaled three words, one of

which was "Adios," which I wished I could say to the congregation.

My husband, Chuck, and I and our friends Howard and Jean Wedell had visited Baja for one purpose: to brighten Christmas for eleven children with a special turkey dinner and lots of gifts.

Their mother, Juana, sensing my dilemma, rose from the expectant audience and joined me at the altar. "I will translate for you."

Great! I thought to myself. *Now all I need is something for you to translate.*

Then a simple story by Ethel Barrett, which I had adapted for Sunday school use many times, came to mind. I told about a good shepherd, his flock of obedient sheep, and a rebel sheep named Blister who got into much trouble.

One night Blister strayed from the flock. He was chased far by a wolf and, in panic, ran until his lungs ached. He fell off a precipice and lay broken in pain and crying on a ledge below. He cried so hard that he lost his voice and could only bleat in hopes that he would attract the attention of his shepherd.

The good shepherd, who hears the faintest bleat or cry, left his ninety-nine other sheep safe and secure, to look for the lost sheep. As he called out for the lamb, he heard Blister's sorrowful bleat and climbed over the cliff. He tore his robe. Thorns cut his head and sharp rocks pierced his hands and feet, but he rescued the broken little lamb and carried him under his warm cloak to the flock and the fold.

"The Lord Jesus is this Good Shepherd," I told my listeners. "You are the lost sheep. Your Shepherd will hear your faintest cry. He is calling you by name this Christmas Day. Jesus will heal your diseases and anoint your eyes and ears with healing ointment. He is ready to heal and restore you and bring you to His Father's fold. Call upon the name of Jesus and be saved. If you would like me to pray for you, just come forward."

Forty individuals, moved by the Holy Spirit, came forward for prayer; many received Jesus as their personal Savior. I was astonished, elated—and then fearful. A woman wearing a shawl came forward with a dark-haired boy; a filthy, adhesive-taped bandage covered one of his eyes. Speaking through Juana, she explained with gestures that much of her son's eye had been destroyed by an accidental shot from a .22-caliber rifle.

My heart went out to this boy and his mother. Not too many years before, my nephew had gone on a camping expedition and had been shot in the eye with a BB gun. He was hospitalized for weeks.

What in the world was the condition of this boy's eye after being hit with a real shell? I wondered. There probably wasn't much eye left.

As the mother continued speaking, I went through all sorts of mental gymnastics. *Maybe I could take the boy to the States to see a doctor,* I thought. And then a practical question dashed that idea to earth: *Where would I get the money to pay hospital and doctor bills for such delicate surgery?* On the heels of that thought came still another: *But no doctor in the world can make a new eye.*

I kept looking into the mother's earnest, brown face as she reminded me, "The señora said that Jesus Christ could heal." Her eyes pleaded with childlike faith for me to produce a miracle in Jesus' name.

I began to squirm, but there was no getting away. The burden was on me and inwardly I cried for help: *Dear God, I can't make an eye. You know I can't make an eye!*

Somewhere in the inner recesses of my soul came a firm response: "But *I* can." And, realizing that this mother had the gift of faith, I laid hands on that child's head and prayed out loud, "Dear God, I can't make an eye, but You can, and I claim a total restoration of sight to this little lamb of Yours. May my hands be the healing hands of Jesus and make him completely whole!"

Nothing seemed to happen, so the mother and her son left for home. The next morning, as we were packing the car to head back to the States, the mother and her son came to see us. The boy's bandage was off. There were no marks on his face or eye!

I hadn't seen the eye under the bandage, but later learned that two reliable witnesses had observed it right after the accident. The bullet had left little behind. Now this precious little boy was indeed whole. Without a doubt, God had worked a Christmas miracle!

Charla Pereau

Charla Pereau is the executive director of Foundation for His Ministry, a Christian outreach organization that provides a home for needy children and offers assistance to families in the Baja region of California and Mexico. Charla has claimed Matthew 10:42 as her mandate for service to others: "Whoever gives one of these little ones only a cup of cold water in the name of a disciple, assuredly, I say to you, he shall by no means lose his reward."

My Father's Christmas Miracle

LINDA STROM

*C*hristmas was a magical event for our family, with fun-filled hours spent decorating the Christmas tree that was nestled in the corner of our living room. Laughter echoed throughout the house, and our love for each other was evident by the happiness we felt spending time together. Yes, Christmas was a magical time.

But that's only because I spent Christmas in the refuge of my imagination. The painful reality of my life was in sharp contrast to my fantasy world. My dad's reputation as an abusive alcoholic filtered throughout the small western Pennsylvania town where we lived, and my mother's despair and inability to change our circumstances crippled her emotionally. With so many townspeople aware of the chaos in our home, shame was my regular childhood companion.

Loneliness was another. I remember walking across the wooden floor of our town's dime store shopping for Christmas gifts. In the background, Christmas carols like "O Little Town of Bethlehem" and "Silent Night" played, producing a bittersweet longing in my heart for the Christ child. He seemed so far away and distant to me, and I felt so alone. There were no silent or holy nights at our house.

Yet in my heart there was a desire for God, a desire planted firmly by the prayers of my grandma Woodworth. She was a pillar of faith to me. "Linda," she would say, "I'm praying for you every day. Remember, God is always greater than anything you'll ever encounter."

Although those words comforted me, God didn't seem any closer as I grew up. Finding myself in an unhappy marriage at twenty-one, and apparently repeating my parents' pattern, I was frightened. Kneeling down one day I cried out, "Oh God, if there is a God, You must help me. I'm so desperate."

That evening Billy Graham spoke on television. While I don't remember exactly what he said, the reality of his words drew my attention and, in response, I asked Jesus Christ to forgive my sins and enter my life. All my emptiness and longing were filled. Within a few months my husband, Dallas, also invited Jesus into his life. As we began to build our life around Him, I understood clearly where my grandmother's strength came from, and began to have hope for my dad. That's the start of my Christmas miracle story.

In 1970, after twenty years of working for the railroad, my dad's job was in jeopardy. The years of drinking had taken its toll on his body, and his life was filled with pain. His dark eyes reflected the sadness in his heart, and the freckles on his face went almost unnoticed as the lines created by years of hard living grooved into his ruddy skin. He wasn't large physically, but he was strong and, to me, handsome.

Although we lived in Minneapolis and Dad still lived in Pennsylvania, he was close to my heart. One of my most ardent prayers was, "Oh Lord, please help my dad. He needs You." A group of women from my church joined me in prayer, and one of them said, "Linda, you need to tell your dad that you love him."

Since intimacy was not a part of our family life, this gesture was a hard thing for me to consider doing. But the prayers continued. One night my father called me. We had our usual unemotional conversation, but at the end there was a pause. I felt the Holy Spirit's nudge and, with all the courage I could muster, said, "Dad, there's something I've wanted to tell you for a long time. I really love you and I'm thankful you're my father." Complete silence followed my words. Then, as my dad said good-bye, I cried tears of joy because what I had spoken to him in faith came from my heart. God had worked a miracle in me!

Tape recorders were popular that Christmas, and after much thought and even some prayer we purchased one. Dallas and I gathered our three boys—ages five, six, and ten—around us and we made a tape for my dad. Each of the boys recited Christmas Scripture verses from our church program along with other special thoughts and wishes. I then shared how the love of Jesus Christ had changed our lives.

On New Year's Eve Dad called and said, "I listened to your tape and it's the best Christmas present I ever received. I'm going to let one of the men who works on the railroad with me listen to it. You know, he's had a lot of the same problems I have."

He also said he was going to come visit us in the spring. What fun we had together. One night we sat at our dinner table, taking turns dipping our forks into the fondue pot. We talked for over an hour.

Since Dad had decided to stay through the weekend, I called our pastor to ask if he would include an extra message in his sermon that Sunday. "Maybe Dad will come to church with us, so tell him everything he needs to know about salvation!"

When Dad said he wouldn't be comfortable in church, my heart sank. Now what should I do? I asked Dallas if he would take our sons and I would stay home with Dad. Again we found ourselves around the kitchen table, talking about different things. Eventually I started sharing with him about Jesus and how He is the way, the truth, and the life. This sharing became an encounter with the living Christ.

Dad said, "I believe everything you are saying. I'm just not ready at this time." Subject closed!

The next summer we began staff training with Campus Crusade for Christ in Arrowhead Springs, California. One morning we were told there was an emergency telephone call from my dad. When I answered the phone, he said, "This isn't an emergency. I just wanted to tell you that when I die I know where I'm going." How we celebrated and rejoiced as a family.

After we returned to Minnesota in the fall, we received another call from Dad. This one to say he had a tumor on his lung. "Don't worry, Linda. I'll be fine," he said. "I'm going to have surgery to remove it." Immediately I knew I should go home and be with my father. We went to the doctor together. He told us Dad had inoperable lung cancer and there was little they could do.

Silence filled the room after the doctor finished. Then Dad spoke, "A year ago I couldn't have handled this, but now I have religion. First my son got religion, then my daughter, and now I have it too. I know God will not give me any more than I can take."

On Sunday we went to church. Dad's once powerful, steady hands trembled. He seemed fearful, wondering if God would forgive him, and if he could ever fully belong to the family of God.

His minister was a gentle, loving man who began regularly visiting my father. As Christmas approached, he encouraged the church choir to go and sing carols at our old farmhouse.

That Christmas is the most memorable of my life. We loaded our car and drove to Pennsylvania to be with Dad, who welcomed us with great joy. Once fearful of their grandpa, our boys began to relax with him. I spent that holiday in awe at the peace God can bring to a situation. Although cancer caused Dad intense pain, I sat with him and read Psalm 23, which enabled him to rest.

Christmas morning, Dad woke us all up. I'm sure he knew

this would be his last Christmas. As we sat watching our sons enjoy their gifts, Dad couldn't wait for me to unwrap the present he'd bought me. Finally, he opened it himself: a brightly colored photo album with flowers and gold lettering. With great emotion he read the inscription, "I thank my God upon every remembrance of you" (Phil. 1:3).

I did see Dad one last time. God made a way for me to get to the hospital in Erie, Pennsylvania, to be with him. I remember feeding him dinner that night. He could no longer hold a fork. I felt so close to him as we prayed together and experienced the father-daughter relationship I had always longed for.

On April 16, 1972, Dad went home to be with the Lord. The Word of God is so true: Jesus can make beauty out of the ashes of our lives. After Dad died, I remembered that long-ago shame I'd felt as a child and thought about how the people in our small town now knew something had happened in our family's life. My brother was a missionary doctor in Africa. My husband and I were on the staff of Campus Crusade for Christ. And many friends had inquired about the changes they saw in Dad's life.

When his pastor gave the eulogy, he mentioned his weekly visits with Dad, and how Communion had become a vital part of their time together. As he offered the Communion elements, my father would kneel to receive them with thanksgiving. As death approached and my father became weaker, the pastor suggested he remain in bed during Communion.

Dad replied, "God waited so long for me, I must get on my knees before Him."

Those words will remain forever in my heart.

Linda Strom

Linda Strom and her husband, Dallas, are the founders of Discipleship Unlimited, a ministry designed "for the equipping of the saints for the work of ministry" (Eph. 4:12). Together they teach others how to conduct marriage seminars, hold weekly interdenominational Bible studies, and coordinate volunteer ministries to inmates in prisons and jails.

Our Christmas Angel

DALE EVANS ROGERS

$\mathscr{D}$uring the Christmas season of 1952 our family was living in Encino, California. The church we attended each Sunday, St. Nicholas's Episcopal, was pastored by Father Harley Wright Smith. Father Smith, who happened to be a bachelor, was loved and admired by many in our community, particularly the single and widowed women in the church.

One Sunday he stood before us and made an unexpected announcement: "Friends, it is with great joy that I announce to you this morning that I have asked Mary to be my bride . . . and she has accepted!"

Well, you should have heard the gossip that began to spread from one corner of our parish to the other, particularly from those who had hoped he would choose them as a companion. You see, Mary was Father Smith's secretary; and she was *much* younger than him.

On the Sunday before Christmas, Father Smith marched solemnly down the aisle reading the story of Christmas as it was recorded by St. Luke. When he got to the passage where an angel appeared to Joseph in a dream and read the line, "Do not be afraid to take Mary as your wife," everyone exploded with laughter. From that day on the entire congregation accepted the engagement of Father Smith and Mary and celebrated their marriage with a huge wedding.

That year was special for our family as well. In August we had suffered the loss of our precious little Robin Elizabeth, our "Angel Unaware." You may know Robin's story. She was born on August 26, 1950—seven and a half pounds and pretty as an angel.

"She's beautiful," Roy declared. He kissed me and said, "Honey, she has little ears like yours!" When I looked at her I saw she had almond-shaped eyes like her daddy's. We were ecstatic.

The next day I began to think that the nurses weren't bringing me my baby nearly as often as they brought other babies to their mothers. When they did bring her, she was sleeping so soundly I couldn't wake her up. The doctors assured me that all was well; they said only that little Robin needed her rest. Whenever I boasted to one of them about how pretty I thought she was or what a fine, healthy child she seemed to be, they changed the subject. On the third day, when I was scheduled to go home, a nurse slipped and said, "Are they going to let you take her home with you?"

"Of course I will take her home with me," I said. I was confused. "Is there any reason why I shouldn't?"

Realizing she had spilled the beans, the nurse turned to leave the room. But she stopped at the door, spun around, and said, "Tell your doctor to tell you the truth." In desperation I called Roy at home.

"I've just found out myself," Roy said in a melancholy voice. "I'll be right there, Maw."

When Roy got to the hospital, the pediatrician told us that Robin had Down's syndrome and that we should consider institutionalizing her. "Her muscle tone is poor, she has problems swallowing, and her heart is defective," he said. "In addition, she's mentally retarded. It would be the best thing for everyone."

"No," Roy said. "We are going home." And that was that. We explained, in very gentle terms, to our children, Dusty and Cheryl, that Robin was not like other babies—that she was very special. They were so good with her. Dusty would spend hours hiding under Robin's bed, playing peek-a-boo and making her laugh. Since Robin was fascinated with music, Cheryl would hold her up to our piano and let her pound the keys.

Why did this happen to us? I wondered. That question haunted me. I thought Robin's affliction might be punishment for my sins—my pride, my ambition, my failures as a mother. Then I thought it might be God's way of speaking to Roy, who always cared so deeply about children. Father Smith told me that he believed Robin came to us with a purpose. "You will learn wonderful lessons from her," he said. "God will guide you."

He was right. That little baby gave us a perspective we had never had before and brought a wonderful peace into our lives. How well I remember the times Roy and I came home after a long, hard day and went straight in to see her. When we played with her and she would smile, our troubles would fall away. She taught us patience and humility; and in the end, she showed us how to be of use to God.

The Lord has many ways of refining people; usually His crucible is fashioned from whatever we hold most dear. In this case, it was our child. Roy, who was once so plagued by the sight of handicapped children in the hospitals he visited that he had questioned God's plan, learned to overcome his skepticism. I learned more than ever to trust His will. What other choice did I have?

One day I came home from work and found doctors at the house. Robin had suffered a series of convulsions, weakening her tremendously. Her legs could not support her any longer. She would never again stand in my lap, and she was too weak now to sit in her stroller and watch the other children play. That Christmas—her second—we gave her a bright red toy piano. It was Dusty's suggestion; he thought she would like playing with it in her crib. Cheryl asked to write Robin's letter to Santa.

Late in August, Robin came down with the mumps. The mumps became encephalitis and the doctors said that if she survived she would no doubt be afflicted with severe brain damage. On Saturday, her temperature rose to 108°. She cried constantly from the pain in her head. We dipped her in ice water to cool her down.

Saturday evening I managed to fall asleep, only to be awakened by a long, deep primeval moan. It was our dog, Lana, scratching at the door of Robin's room. Lana wailed and howled and paced through the night as Robin weakened and slipped into unconsciousness.

Sunday evening, Robin's heart gave out. Her room was filled with gifts and new toys, waiting to be played with. But there would be no party on August 26. Robin's second birthday would be the day we put her in the ground.

The day after Robin's funeral we left for New York for a concert at Madison Square Garden. It had been scheduled months before and there were too many people counting on us to let our sorrow get in the way. On the way to the train for New York, we drove past Forest Lawn Cemetery. There was an illuminated cross on top of the mausoleum where Robin had been laid to rest. I thought of her little body in there and a great sense of loss welled up in me. When we boarded the train, I wept for an hour.

In my unending grief over Robin, something Roy had said at the funeral kept running through my mind: "She looks like a small-size sleeping angel." I recalled a verse from the thirteenth chapter of Hebrews: "Be not forgetful to entertain strangers: for thereby some have entertained angels unawares" (v. 2 KJV).

Like sunlight breaking clouds after a storm of darkness, it all became clear to me. I knew what Robin's life meant and I saw what I had to do. She had come to us from God—an angel—with all her handicaps and frailties to make us aware that His strength is found in weakness. In the two years she had been with us we had grown close as a family, and we had learned how deeply we needed to depend on God. I knew that my job was to deliver that message to others.

On Christmas Eve, before attending that eventful service at St. Nicholas's where Father Smith made his "angelic" announcement about Mary, we trimmed a lovely Christmas tree in our front room. We placed a white, shimmering angel at the top and named her "Angel Robin."

At the service my eyes were riveted on the statue of the Virgin Mary holding her infant son, the Christ child. So much had happened since Robin had gone to her heavenly home. Roy and I had adopted two beautiful children—a seven-month-old from Hope Cottage in Dallas, and a five-year-old foster child from Kentucky. And so much lay ahead. I would soon tell Robin's story to the world in the book *Angel Unaware*.

But for now I sat with glistening eyes, staring at the blessed mother of our Lord. It was because of her son that my precious little daughter was now safe and joyful and perfect for eternity. It was because Jesus gave His life on the cross that everyone who accepts Him will one day be made whole and all of our earthly sorrows will forever disappear. I can hear Robin say, "I'm perfectly all right, now that I'm rid of that lump of hindering clay. . . . And now, Father, please . . . could I just go out and try my wings?"

Dale Evans Rogers

In the 1940s and 1950s Dale Evans Rogers and her husband, Roy Rogers, were the popular singing stars of countless western television programs and movies. Their signature song, "Happy Trails," represented the wholesome ideals and strong moral values they shared with fans around the world. Today Dale Evans keeps busy with a variety of endeavors, including The Roy Rogers–Dale Evans Museum and a talk show on the Trinity Broadcasting Network. Portions of this article were adapted from Happy Trails: Our Life Story *(Simon & Schuster, 1994).*

CHAPTER 24

A Special Christmas Day

EVELYN ROBERTS

*C*hristmas has always been a special day in our family, just as it is in the hearts and homes of Christians around the world. In our case, however, it has added significance because it is also the day Oral and I celebrate our wedding anniversary. Yes, we were married on December 25, 1938.

The Roberts family likes to mark special occasions with a big, hearty meal. Since Christmas is the grandest celebration of the year, we start the festivities with a huge breakfast of country ham, hot biscuits, scrambled eggs, gravy, and sorghum molasses. After the last biscuit has been buttered and the orange juice has disappeared, except for a pulpy residue in the pitcher, we let our eager grandchildren rush in to open the presents—just as their parents did years before. We spend the rest of the day enjoying the fellowship of our family by reading the Christmas story from the gospel of St. Luke, testifying about the ways God has blessed us through the year, and praying for the partners of our ministry.

Although the details of each Christmas have become fuzzy over the years as one precious memory builds upon another, there is one memory that is embedded in my heart. It is the Christmas of 1976, the last holiday season we enjoyed with our daughter Rebecca.

Rebecca Ann Roberts was born December 16, 1939. She was a beautiful child with the dark Native American features and flowing hair of her father. She had an outgoing personality and was, according to her father, a "mama's girl."

For the first three years of her life she traveled with us as we held our revival meetings. She said her first words, cut her first teeth, and took her first steps in the homes of the pastors who sponsored us around the country. They all loved her dearly.

Rebecca was also a bright student with a quick mind. In fact, when she was in high school, I switched her from one school to another because she seemed to be getting all A's without working very hard. She eventually graduated with a B average and went to the University of Tulsa.

While our children were growing up, Oral was gone much of the time for his healing crusades. One day, after he had returned from a lengthy trip, he asked what the children had been up to during his absence. I started with Rebecca and told him that she had said, "Mother, I'll never be a student. All I really want to do is have a career. I want to work in Dad's office."

"What did you tell her?" Oral asked.

"I was waiting to see how you felt about it."

"Well," Oral replied, "I think she's described herself very well. She's a strong young woman, she loves the Lord, and she'll make some good young Christian man a great wife."

"Then you better get ready," I said. "She's fallen in love with Marshall, the son of Reverend W. J. Nash. I think they're going to get married; Marshall is waiting to ask you for her hand when you get the time."

Oral freely gave consent for Marshall to marry Rebecca. They had a lovely wedding ceremony in our front yard. She was a beautiful bride.

Over the next few years Marshall became a successful businessman in the Tulsa area, and he and Rebecca had three lovely children. Oral and I were thrilled to be grandparents and were happy to see Rebecca so fulfilled in her life. We spent our last Christmas with her in 1976.

But now its Christmas and, again, my thoughts return to 1976. It was a typically cool December day in Oklahoma, with temperatures in the thirties. We built a roaring fire in the fireplace and ate our usual big breakfast. After we had opened presents and eaten Christmas dinner, we sat down for our traditional time of reflection.

When it was Rebecca's turn, she paused and said something I will never forget. Her exact words were: "I have never known— *really* known—who I am. First, I was known as Oral Roberts's daughter. Then as Marshall's wife. Then as the mother of Brenda,

Marcia, and Jon. But now, today, at last I know who I am and where I'm going."

None of us knew at the time that we would never share another Christmas with Rebecca and Marshall.

Early on a Friday morning in 1977, our doorbell rang. It was our dear friend and associate, Collins Steele. His face was ashen.

"I have some bad news," he said. "Marshall and Rebecca died last night in a plane crash over Kansas on their way to Tulsa. I'm so sorry."

I shook as if I had a chill, and then it struck me. "Oh the children! They'll be up by this time, waiting for Mommy and Daddy to come home."

We threw on some clothes and rushed over to Rebecca and Marshall's home. When we rang the doorbell, all three children ran to the door, expecting to find their parents. Instead, they saw us. They knew something was wrong when they saw the tears in our eyes. "Children," Oral said, "Mommy and Daddy are not coming home. They were killed a few hours ago when their plane crashed." We sat there, hugging them, crying and trying to hold on emotionally.

The days and weeks and months ahead were difficult and there were times when I didn't think I would be able to make it through the day. Yet, God was faithful and we were comforted by the kind words and prayers of friends and strangers alike. Marshall's brother, Bill, and his wife, Edna, raised those three precious little children and were wonderful parents. Today all three are successful and happy young people who have committed their lives to the Lord.

That Christmas of 1976, none of us knew that our next "homecoming" celebration with our dear children would be the day we stand in that bright land where there is no sorrow and all tears have been wiped away.

But God knew, and He graciously gave us one last celebration together. And, until our glorious reunion, Rebecca's words will remain in my heart: "Today, at last I know who I am and where I'm going."

Evelyn Lutman Roberts

Evelyn Lutman Roberts and her husband, evangelist Oral Roberts, are the founders of Oral Roberts University. Evelyn has written several books, including His Darling Wife, Evelyn *and* Heaven Has a Floor, *a children's book. She attended Northeastern State University in Oklahoma and Texas College of Arts and Industries in Kingsville, Texas. Evelyn and Oral are the parents of four children, thirteen grandchildren, and one great-grandchild.*

PART THREE

CREATING
THE MEMORIES OF

Christmas

Future

IDEAS
FOR CHRISTMASES
TO COME

Our
Christmas Crèches

TERRY MEEUWSEN

*J*ust the thought of Christmas brings a smile to my lips and a feeling of celebration to my heart. It's a time when the whole world seems to hover in anticipation. Even those who do not share the Christian faith are impacted in some way by the spirit of the season. Houses are outlined with colorful Christmas lights, Christmas carols can be heard almost everywhere you go, the smell of cinnamon and pine trees tingles the noses of those who come near. Christmas is literally a feast for the senses!

I know some people bemoan the fact that the Christmas season seems to begin earlier and earlier each year, but I am not one of them. Oh, to be sure, I dislike all the commercialism and slick promotion as much as anyone. But the fun of receiving cards and pictures from far-away friends, baking traditional goodies, and basking in the late evening peacefulness of a room lit only by a flickering fire and a twinkling Christmas tree far outweigh any of the hassles and pressures.

Having four children in the house definitely adds something special to the holiday season. I've given considerable thought and effort to continuing traditions from the childhoods my husband

and I enjoyed as well as establishing "new traditions" of our own. One of our favorite new holiday traditions is to collect Christmas crèches. Though the children help me set them up, most of them are fragile and not to be handled by little hands. A few years back, when my children were all toddlers, I decided we needed a manger scene and a baby Jesus they could touch as much as they wanted. I found some unpainted wooden figures for a simple manger, bought some paints and brushes, and spent a quiet evening painting figures that I hoped would become beloved Christmas keepsakes. Later, in a country store, I found a rustic little stable made by a retired pastor, which was just the right size for those little wooden figures.

One night we gathered on our knees at the coffee table in the family room to put together our "childproof" manger scene. Drew, my oldest son, put Joseph in place. Tory, my daughter, carefully placed Mary next to him. My son J. P. piped up, "Hey Mom, don't foh-get those thwee wise guys!" (I've never been able to see the wise men again without thinking of them as "those three wise guys!")

Over the years that little manger scene has been arranged and rearranged a thousand different times. During the holiday season, late in the evening when I'm able to finally sit down to a cup of tea, I'll glance over at the coffee table and chuckle. Sometimes the three wise guys are on the roof. Occasionally the sheep are standing on their heads. And sometimes the figures have all been lined up like dominoes and then knocked down. The little gate on the stable kind of sags on its hinges because it's been opened and closed so many times. Even our dog has left teeth marks on one of the sheep.

But I love the fingerprints and scratches and nicks that cover those small figures. I know that little hands and tender hearts have knelt before that coffee table manger and thought about the awesome night when the Creator of the universe became a little baby so we could touch Him and love Him and receive Him into our own hearts and lives. One year a little baby became a special part of our Christmas celebration.

CELEBRATING THE GIFT OF A SPECIAL BABY

Both of our younger boys are adopted and both are very special answers to prayer. One of our Christmas traditions is to send a Christmas letter and family picture to all of our friends at Christmastime. The year we adopted Tyler I began to reflect on the Scripture that joyfully declares "unto us a Child is born, unto us a Son is given." With awe in my heart I realized that we would experience this verse that Christmas in two different ways— spiritually, as we celebrated Jesus, and physically, with Tyler's first Christmas in our family.

That summer a gem of an idea began to take shape. I thought it would be wonderful if we could create a living manger scene with our children that would celebrate the birth of our Savior while rejoicing in the addition of another child, Tyler, to our family.

During a visit with my mother- and father-in-law I noticed a rustic wooden sawhorse they had set at the end of their driveway to be picked up with the trash. To me it looked just like a manger, and soon my husband was patiently clearing a place for it in the back of our van.

Next I enlisted the aid of my mom who had creatively sewn costumes and clothing for her children and grandchildren for years. I described my idea to her and we had a wonderful time shopping for fabric. She caught the vision and was soon off and running with her trusty sewing machine.

J. P., who is Korean, wanted to be one of the wise men. As I glued faux jewels onto a gold cardboard crown for him, I thought, *Not every family has their very own wise man from the East!*

By autumn we had finished our planning. With a bale of hay in the trunk we headed for the studio of a *very* patient photographer friend. That Christmas our friends received a letter announcing Tyler's arrival and a photo of our very own family manger scene.

Even though our children have grown beyond their toddler years, the memories return in a rush whenever I set up one of those manger scenes. I often stop and privately take a moment to celebrate the incredible gift of God's love. "Do not be afraid, for behold, I bring you good tidings of great joy which will be to all people. For there is born to you this day in the city of David a Savior, who is Christ the Lord. And this will be the sign to you: You will find a Babe wrapped in swaddling clothes, lying in a manger" (Luke 2:10–12).

This is not a book of crafts or "how-to" ideas; it's a collection of special memories. Memories, remember, are more often created from *doing* than they are from *observing*. The stories that follow offer practical and spiritually uplifting ideas for making every Christmas special.

I'd like to begin this part with one of my grandmother's recipes for Norwegian cookies, which I mentioned earlier as one of my childhood memories of Christmas.

Norwegian Dessert Rosettes

2 eggs, slightly beaten	1 cup milk
2 tsp. sugar	1 cup flour
1/4 tsp. salt	1 Tbsp. lemon extract

Add sugar to slightly beaten eggs, then add milk. Sift flour before measuring, then together with salt. Stir into first mixture and beat until smooth (about the consistency of heavy cream). Add flavoring and fry as directed with a rosette iron.

USE OF ROSETTE IRON

Place approximately 3" of oil in deep fryer or saucepan and heat to 375°.

Securely attach desired rosette forms on the twin handle and immerse in oil until thoroughly heated. Lift iron out, shaking off excess oil, and dip into prepared batter. Dip only to depth of the form, not over the top of it as excess batter will have to be removed after baking before rosettes can be taken off forms. Dip forms into the hot oil. When foamy bubbling stops and/or rosettes are a delicate brown, lift iron out of oil, allowing excess oil to drip off iron back into fryer, and remove the rosette cookies. (You may have to tap the top of each form with a wooden spoon to make cookie release.)

Continue cooling on paper towels, open side down so excess oil will run out. Reheat iron as necessary in the hot oil before making more rosettes.

When cool, or before serving, sprinkle with powdered or granulated sugar.

Note: The process may take some practice! If iron or oil is not the correct temperature (either too hot or too cold), batter will not adhere to the forms. If rosettes are not crisp, the batter is too thick and should be diluted with milk.

CHAPTER 25

The Year My Father Brought Me Christmas

WIN COUCHMAN

*R*emember the Grinch who almost stole Christmas? Dr. Seuss was kind enough to warn us about that critter. But I have discovered a whole tribe of grinches, and several of them have given me enormous grief over the years.

For instance there is the *Time Grinch*. Early in the year he hangs on the wall looking like an innocent calendar. But before you know it, he has dropped all his pages but one. Suddenly he has a leering face and two hands that race round and round as he mutters *tick, tick, tick*.

To keep the Time Grinch from stealing Christmas, you must deal in reality. We each have different metabolisms, hormones, budgets, and number of children (or no children), and while some people have excess energy, for others a hyper-holiday routine spells disaster.

Ask yourself, What one experience of Christmas can I *not* do without? Whatever it is, you have to make time for it. For me it is the expression of childlike wonder. When I rush around and lose the *wonder* of God sending His Son to earth as a baby, well, I lose what really matters to me about Christmas. So I only send cards to people I never see (trying to make sure that the people I love and do see get special greetings and hugs when our paths cross). I have given up trying to change anyone's life with a perfect gift. And I am picky about the number of parties I attend.

Among the other grinches that have troubled my life, the *Secular Grinch* stands out. He is that nine-foot-tall inflatable Santa who rides into town the day after Halloween. When our children were young, we let them enjoy the fairy-tale story of Santa, but only in moderation. We read *The Night Before Christmas* together, but we stayed away from malls and didn't let them sit on Santa's lap. We chose wrappings and cards that didn't feature the jolly old elf since, at our house, he was not the gift bringer. Now that we are older and have grandchildren, we still politely ignore him. Instead, we encourage them to read books and listen to music about baby Jesus.

We didn't want to demean the old fellow, but we tried to minimize his part in our celebrations and to focus rather on the Savior. The highlight of our Christmas holidays was to hold a yearly birthday party for Jesus where each of our children memorized and recited a portion of the Christmas story.

Santa is cute as a fairy tale, but I certainly wish people

wouldn't make him an article of faith. Although he seems benign, he confuses children. He really is a type of "religious" figure whose theology is "Do good, get rewarded. Do bad, get punished." Little children, during their most formative years, get mixed up by this godlike fellow who knows nothing of acceptance by faith alone.

One Christmas Eve, when our son Donny was four, I heard him crying in his room. Since he had been in such a good mood before bed, I rushed in to see what was the matter. Through his choking sobs he told me that he had forgotten to get the Birthday Boy a gift. When I asked him what he thought Jesus wanted, he said, "He wants me."

I sat in silent awe beside him while he took care of this eternally important transaction. Donny's young conversion encouraged me to keep on emphasizing the birth of Jesus as the absolute center of our Christmas celebrations.

Another grinch that can impinge on the spiritual heart of Christmas is the *Traditions Grinch*. He says only one phrase: "But we've always done it this way." Somehow his voice comes through with such parental authority it is hard not to allow him to steal the true meaning of Christmas.

Don't get me wrong; I'm a firm believer in celebrating the holidays. In fact, God invented celebration. The entire book of Leviticus is an outline for ways God's people, Israel, were to commemorate and enjoy holy days. As these celebrations were passed down to the Christian era, they were personalized by different regions of the world. While these changes were inevitable, the problem often is that our own traditions are given a "god-weight." When the Traditions Grinch says, "But we've always done it this way!" or "We've always opened our gifts on Christmas Eve!" or "You've always come home for Christmas!" he speaks with an air of mock authority. But don't worry, he isn't the voice of God. As each generation matures, and new families form, some cherished traditions need to be reconsidered.

One year a particularly horrid grinch showed up to wreck my holiday, and I almost let him do it. I'll call him the *Circumstance Grinch*. My darling husband was newly home after fourteen months in the Korean War, and I wanted our Christmas to be perfect.

But when our two little children leaned against me on Christmas Eve, whimpering over hurting tummies, I knew we were in for a letdown. I called my parents and told them our children had the flu and that we would not be at the family gathering the next day. My fantasy lay broken before me. The leering Circumstance Grinch begged for his favorite food: self-pity. I gave him plenty, and took a double batch to bed myself.

On Christmas morning, just before dawn, I was awakened from a deep sleep by a hauntingly familiar sound. I sat straight up in bed and listened closely. It was the song of my father's old Model A pickup.

I jumped out of bed, pulled on my robe, and ran through our farmhouse to the front porch just as my dad drove into the yard. As I reached to open his door, he waved me away.

"Merry Christmas, honey," he said cheerfully. "Don't come near me. I don't want your flu bugs. I just came to bring your presents."

I backed away and he got out, let down the tailgate, and handed me a pile of gifts, which I carried up the steps to the porch. As I turned for one last present I noticed he was standing there, grinning his Irish grin, with his hands behind his back. "I thought you might want this too," he said. I couldn't believe it; he was holding the top *half* of Mother's and his Christmas tree! Its tinsel fluttered in the soft morning breeze, and as I took it I sobbed. He waved his arm, hopped back into his pickup, and drove off toward home.

I stood looking at his precious, crazy gift, thinking how ridiculous the bottom half of my parents' tree was going to look the rest of the holiday season. My father gave the essence of Christmas with that gesture of love.

Years later, long after my father had passed away, I started thinking about that chilly morning and suddenly realized that in some ways everything about it parallels the story of Christmas. God wants me to come "home" some day too. But first I need to be cured of my "sin" bug. Just as Daddy didn't want to catch the flu from me, God will not allow heaven to be polluted with my selfishness, my pride, or my rebellion.

Yet, because God loved me, He sent His Son, the Star of Heaven, to be a sacrifice for my sins and the sins of the world. Our precious Savior said, "I'll go to earth. I'll let them know You love them. And I'll take care of their sin problem too. I'll die for them so they can be forgiven and recreated."

And, just like that Christmas tree, He came to earth and was cut off. Yet, today He shines brighter than the sun and someday I will bask in His presence for eternity.

Win Couchman

Win Couchman grew up in California on a prune-and-walnut ranch. Today she and her husband, Bob, live in Wisconsin where Win is a writer, teacher, speaker, and lay counselor. Following Bob's retirement ten years ago, the Couchmans became staff members for International Teams, a missions organization active in church planting and other ministries of mercy around the world. Win has written a book and two study guides on small groups, as well as a memoir called Don't Call Me Spry.

My Tribute

ANNE GRAHAM LOTZ

*E*ach year as I approach the Christmas holidays, I ask the King what He would like for His birthday. He is very creative in His suggestions! They vary widely but have one thing in common: The gift is always sacrificial in nature, something I *would* not do except the King requested it. And it is something I *could* not do except the King enabled me.

Perhaps the most difficult gift the Lord seemed to ask of me was to carry out the dying request of an executed murderer. Velma Barfield was convicted of four murders, including that of her own mother. But, praise God, during her prison sentence she accepted Christ as her Savior and became a radically transformed believer. Many people who had witnessed the change in Velma's life, including the prison warden and guards, wanted the governor to grant her a pardon. However, the families of the victims fought the possibility, and the pardon was denied.

Before her execution, Velma asked me if I would deliver her letters of apology to each of the victims' families. With great apprehension, I personally delivered the letters to each family — only to be emphatically rejected. In reflection, afterward, I felt that the Lord had given me a small glimpse of what it was like for Him to deliver a positive message of hope and forgiveness when He came that first Christmas, yet was rejected and despised. I experienced deep joy to think I had shared a small portion of His suffering.

Not all the gifts to the King are this difficult to fulfill. But the increased degree of difficulty increases the degree of joy in giving since the only reason I would give it is because the King asked.

The apostle Paul understood the meaning of costly giving. But he also was well acquainted with the enabling power of the Holy Spirit to overcome human frailties and achieve the King's desire. In his second letter to the troubled church at Corinth, Paul speaks in deeply personal terms to his readers to sacrificially give to Him:

> *And now, brothers, we want you to know about the grace that God has given the Macedonian churches. Out of the most severe trial, their overflowing joy and their extreme poverty welled up in rich generosity. For I testify that they gave as much as they were able, and even beyond their ability. . . . And they did not do as we expected, but they*

gave themselves first to the Lord and then to us in keeping with God's will. (2 Cor. 8:1–3, 5 NIV)

God wants us to give freely out of our love for Him as an act of worship. Sometimes the gift He asks of us is quite simple. One year I distinctly felt Him leading me to add to my already completed speaking engagements. Normally I stay home in December and January to be with my family over the holidays. At the end of November that year, I was asked to replace a speaker at three large conferences in California during the next few weeks before Christmas. Just as I was about to tell the organizer I regretfully would have to decline her invitation, I felt the Lord urging me to accept her offer as my gift to Him that year.

I don't know specifically why He felt this was an important task for me to fulfill. The source of my joy was not in the result or the impact the gift had on others, but in the very act of giving the King a gift He desired.

In fact, during one holiday season I felt no specific leading from the Holy Spirit toward a gift for Him. I kept waiting and listening for a word or sign but I never received it. That year I felt a real sense of emptiness in my spirit. I kept asking myself, *Did I miss His gift suggestion and therefore have nothing to give the King for His birthday?*

Therefore, each year, with humility, I thank the King when He reveals His gift suggestion to me. And I offer it to Him as my tribute with love! The blessing I receive is the joy of entering into the true meaning of Christmas. Because on that first Christmas morning, God gave us a gift with the highest degree of difficulty as an expression of His love for us.

I pray that this Christmas you will ask the King for His gift suggestion. When He impresses on your heart the gift He desires, offer it to Him as your tribute with love!

Anne Graham Lotz

Anne Graham Lotz was born in Mon-treat, North Carolina, the second daugh-ter of Billy and Ruth Graham. She is the wife of Dr. Dan Lotz, and the mother of three children. From 1976 until 1988 Anne taught a Bible class called Bible Study Fellowship in her hometown. More than five hundred women regularly attended her weekly lessons. Her original class multiplied several times until today there are nine other classes of similar size in Raleigh. In 1988, Anne established AnGeL Ministries, a non-profit organization that provides Bible study resources and coordinates her speaking schedule. Portions of this article were adapted from The Vision of His Glory *(Word Publishing, 1996).*

CHAPTER 27

A Christmas Treat

DEDE ROBERTSON

*C*hristmas at the Robertson home centers around the birth of our Savior, Jesus Christ. We have an old crèche made from window-shade rollers and slates that was given to me by my aunt Elze and uncle Emmett the year I discovered there wasn't a Santa Claus. They owned a window-shade factory and had one of their talented workers make it for me. The figurines were created in Germany of delicately painted porcelain. All have survived many moves, and even a fire, with only a few lost sheep and some broken heads, which were easily repaired with a little glue.

Dressing the house in its Christmas finery is a project for the whole family. When our children were young we lived near a wood, and the boys would select and cut green boughs and holly to spread throughout the house. Then Pat would take all the children in search of the perfect tree, which they would chop down, drag through the snow to our house, and anchor in its stand.

Several days prior to setting up the tree, we would string popcorn and cranberry strands for a colorful garland. After we draped the lights, everyone began placing our many ornaments on the tree. Some were very old, some were homemade, and some were new—but they were all special to us. When the tree was finished, it was time for hot-mulled cider and cookies.

After our traditional supper of scalloped oysters (a natural for residents of Tidewater, Virginia), chicken salad, ham biscuits, ambrosia, and orange date nut bread, we would gather around the piano to sing Christmas carols and share stories with one another. Soon Pat would pick up his Bible, and we would gather around him as he read from the second chapter of Luke, the glorious account of that very first Christmas, the birth of our Lord and Savior, Jesus Christ. Afterward the children were encouraged to share what this event has meant in their lives. Pat would close with a prayer of praise and thanksgiving for God's love and the many blessings He had bestowed upon us during the year.

Then came the big moment! Earlier we had set up the manger scene without the baby Jesus. Now our youngest child would have the privilege of placing the baby in the manger. The first to do this was Tim, who soon surrendered the privilege to Elizabeth, then Gordon, and finally to Ann, who carried on the

tradition until our grandchildren were born: Laura, then Elizabeth, Catherine, Willis, Charlie, Caroline, Christina, Emily,
Abby, Evelyn, and, this year, Patrick. There will be a new one by
next Christmas, so Patrick won't have the honor for long!

What a joy it is to watch the little ones' eyes light up as
everyone offers words of encouragement. Oh, the tender care
that is given to the proper placement of that tiny figurine! I know
it's merely a tradition—and, yes, even a ritual—but it has helped
instill the all-encompassing love of God for each one of us into
our children's and grandchildren's hearts.

The old ornaments have made way for new ones over the
years. I took up painting some time ago, and now my tree is
covered with hand-decorated angels. Each grandchild has
picked his or her favorite and, when they marry, I will give it to
them to begin their own collection.

I love the contrast of the angels and the glories of heaven
with the humble little crèche. Most of all, I love the warm fuzzy
feeling I get when all my family is gathered at our home,
worshiping and praising our wonderful Lord and Savior.

As my special gift to you, please try my recipe for orange
date nut bread. I hope your family will enjoy it as much as ours!

Orange Date Nut Bread

1 cup butter or margarine	1/4 cup orange juice
2 cups sugar	1 cup buttermilk
4 eggs	Grated rind of 1 orange
3 cups sifted flour	1 cup chopped nuts
1 1/2 tsp. baking soda	1 cup chopped dates

1 tsp. salt

1/4 cup chopped nuts for top of cake

Preheat oven to 350°. In a large bowl, cream sugar and butter together. Add eggs one at a time, beating after each addition. Blend flour, salt, baking soda, and sift together. Add buttermilk and orange juice alternately to egg mixture. Fold in orange rind, nuts, and dates (which have been dredged with flour) to the batter. Pour into greased and floured pan, making one angel cake pan or two loaf pans. Bake at 350° for one hour.

Remove from the oven. Let cool for 20 minutes and turn out on rack. While still warm, pour a glaze of 1 grated orange rind, 1 cup sugar, 1 cup orange juice heated until sugar dissolves, over cake's top and sides.

Adelia Elmer "Dede" Robertson

Adelia Elmer "Dede" Robertson is the wife of Dr. M. G. "Pat" Robertson, founder and chief executive officer of The Christian Broadcasting Network, Inc. Dede was born in Columbus, Ohio, graduated from Ohio State University in 1949 with a degree in social administration, and received a master of nursing degree from Yale University in 1955. While attending Yale, she met Pat Robertson, then a student in the Yale Law School. They were married in 1954. Dede is the mother of two sons and two daughters. She was hostess of a television program, "Lifeline," from 1961 to 1964 and has written two books, My God Will Supply and The New You. She serves on the board of trustees of Regent University, is a board member and secretary of CBN, and is a board member of Physicians for Peace.

CHAPTER 28

The Ever-Ready Christmas Tree

LIZ CURTIS HIGGS

In our family, each Christmas is defined by one specific memory—the Christmas I made smoked turkey without meaning to, the year I gave everyone their gifts in brown paper bags, the Christmas Day we spent on the Pennsylvania Turnpike. But 1992 will always be remembered as the year I received a ten-foot artificial Christmas tree—decorated from top to bottom—as an honorarium for speaking at a local charitable organization. Usually we make a trip to a nearby tree farm and cut down our own fragrant spruce, but we were in the process of moving, so a ready-to-go tree was a welcome gift.

One afternoon early that December, while I was in the middle of painting the dining room ceiling in our new home, the phone call came: "Mrs. Higgs, we're ready to deliver your tree."

"Great!" I said, my voice bouncing off the bare walls. "How about next Wednesday around three o'clock?"

The caller was silent for a moment, then said, "Uh, Mrs. Higgs, I'm calling you from a car phone. We're a block away from your house."

"Are you kidding?!" I exclaimed, backing down the ladder. They were not. Minutes later, a delivery truck pulled into our drive. As I hurried out to direct traffic, the tree was unloaded, shrouded in plastic wrap. It was enormous.

"Where do you want it?" was their logical question.

"Let's just put it in the garage for now," I suggested, pointing the way.

Two fullback-size fellas grunted and sweated as they dragged our tree toward the garage. *Gee*, I thought, *it sure looks heavy*. Finally, they gave the tree a mighty yank and the ornamental giant landed just inside the garage door.

Nearly a week passed, and our house was beginning to look like a home. "It's probably about time we bring in the Christmas tree," I casually mentioned to my husband, Bill, one evening.

He looked puzzled. "What tree?" he asked.

"Remember that free tree I was given? It's just inside the garage door. C'mon, I'll hold the door and you can carry it in."

Shaking his head, Bill pulled on his coat and headed out into the night. The garage door swooshed open, and then I heard a distinct groan, "Liz-z-zz!" I grabbed my own coat and made tracks for the garage.

It was not a pretty sight. Cinnamon sticks, once neatly tied with bright red ribbons on the tree, dangled forlornly, having served as a holiday lunch for some hungry squirrels that had chewed through the plastic wrap. A stray cat had celebrated the season by knocking off mice-size ornaments that had rolled from one end of our garage to another. The angel perching on the ten-foot treetop drooped sideways, obviously ashamed of what had transpired below.

"Oh, Bill!" I moaned, my eyes stinging with tears. "Is it hopeless?"

"Well, it'll take some effort to make the tree look nice again," he said, picking up a glass ball that had survived the cat-astrophe.

"No problem," I assured him. "I found a box of ornaments yesterday, so we'll have plenty to work with. Think you can carry it in?"

What man in his macho mind would say, "No, it's too heavy for me"? Bill was no exception. He valiantly bent down, grabbed it at the base, and pulled. It moved a fraction of an inch. Another pull yielded almost an inch. Progress. Two more yanks brought it another two inches farther along. Bill straightened up. "Did one man move this in here?" he asked, wiping his brow.

"No, two men," I answered reluctantly. "Big guys." Bill was not comforted by this news. "I can help," I offered, grabbing the trunk halfway up. "You take the bottom, and I'll take the top." Which is exactly what I did. Took the top right off the tree.

Never having owned an artificial tree, I didn't know they came apart. You haven't lived till you've tried to steer five feet of heavily decorated Christmas tree back into an opening the size of a pencil. With one hand. And with one husband jumping up and down, shouting instructions. It got very old, very fast.

"Here, you try it!" I said, exasperated, giving him room to reach through the prickly branches and grab hold of the trunk. Between us, we managed to get the tree back together. Above us, even the angel looked grateful. "Okay," I said, standing back, "there must be a better way."

Scooting some discarded cardboard under the tree, we finally were able to drag it through the door and onto the driveway. It took us fifteen minutes to move it all of three feet. I looked up to see two noses pressed against the kitchen window as our children watched us move the tree down the driveway, then across the front yard. Had a camera been handy to capture the moment, you would have seen Bill with a Christmas tree lying across his back, me hanging on to the base for dear life, going backward up the (thankfully) short flight of steps to our front porch.

A new problem became immediately apparent: Our ten-foot tree was four feet wide with ornaments; our eight-foot front door was three feet wide with hinges. "We go in backward," Bill announced. I winced as the sound of breaking glass and squishing cranberries greeted our ears.

"Pull in your tummy!" I shouted to the tree as a final heave-ho brought it suddenly into the foyer of our farmhouse.

Bill dropped to the foot of the steps, as the kids danced around in excitement. "Okay," he said wearily, "where do you want it?"

My mind went blank. "I haven't the faintest idea," I finally confessed, looking down the hall and through the doorways around us. "There are boxes in every single room except the kitchen. It's big enough, I guess. Want to drag it there?"

The hall rug was a big help as we headed east. Two more doorways dislodged a few more ornaments, but soon the tree stood more or less straight in the exact center of the kitchen. The angel now soared above the ceiling fan, and I cautioned the kids that under no circumstances was the fan to be turned on.

After hustling our wide-eyed elves off to bed, Bill and I spent an hour whipping the tree into shape. The damage wasn't as bad as we had feared, and once the broken decorations were replaced with some old favorites, the tree looked spiffy again. Relieved that we had accomplished our task, we crawled off to bed.

The Christmas tree spent several days in our kitchen. At first, every time I came around the corner, I jumped back at the sight of it standing there, quietly taking up half the room. But as Christmas grew closer, we grew accustomed to the green giant in the kitchen, and acted surprised when friends walked in and did a double take. "What is *that*?" they would say. "A Christmas tree, of course," we would answer. "Don't you have one?"

But finally, it became unhandy to have it in the center of the busiest room in the house, so we looked for a new location. "There are fewer boxes in the downstairs bedroom," I suggested. "How 'bout there?" Another two doorways to maneuver, and the tree had a new venue. Now when friends asked us if we still had a Christmas tree in our kitchen, we smiled brightly and said, "Oh, no! It's in the front bedroom."

A few days later, however, the tree was transported to the

family room while I finished decorating the bedroom for guests. That move involved going down a step, plus avoiding a ceiling fan that was accidentally activated. But the tree showed great staying power. The only room on the first floor it didn't visit was the bathroom—but that was only because of logistics.

By Christmas Eve, it had its final resting place: the dining room. A bit worse for wear but still a glorious sight, it fit perfectly in the corner. We hadn't lost a single twinkling bulb in all that hauling around, and the angel stood proudly at the helm, looking up at a freshly painted ceiling just inches above her halo.

When Bill's parents and grandmother arrived for our traditional bowl of homemade soup and bread, we hurried them in to see our tree. "It's lovely!" my mother-in-law exclaimed.

"It was free," my son Matthew declared proudly. Like his father, he appreciated a good bargain.

Three-year-old Lillian, her eyes full of wonder, said, "Our tree has lived in every room, but this is her favorite!"

My in-laws looked at me for an explanation, but I just smiled. "That's true," I said. "Some trees are pickier than others."

Our first Christmas in our new home went without a hitch. When New Year's Day arrived—traditionally the day for taking down a cut Christmas tree and sweeping up the dried needles—I had a sudden burst of inspiration. This tree would never lose its needles. I could enjoy it right through Epiphany!

By mid-January, still cozy in its corner of the dining room, the tree continued to look fresh and green—though a tad off-season. I removed all the Yuletide ornaments and left only the twinkling lights and white snowflakes on its branches. "It's a January tree," I informed the family, and there the tree stayed.

When February came along, it seemed appropriate to replace the snowflakes with valentines, so the kids and I had a blast covering the tree with paper hearts. *Not every family has a Valentine's tree*, I thought warmly.

Frankly, the shamrocks in March got lost amid all the green, so on the first of April we moved quickly to Easter eggs of every hue and multicolored grass dripping from the branches. It was my favorite month so far.

Friends were less impressed. When my in-laws came for Easter dinner, they took one look and said, "Well!"

By May, it was getting harder to keep the branches dust-free, and, though lovely, sunflowers couldn't overcome the Christmas-in-July look. Visitors rolled their eyes and even the kids wearied of explaining to people that "Mom thought it would be fun to have a holiday tree all year."

By August, the tree was history: a two-piece memory shoved back in the corner of the garage, where it all began.

November rolled around, and it was time for my annual holiday presentation to the charitable organization that started it all. With their request for my speaking services came their generous offer: "Liz, may we give you another tree this year?"

"No thanks," I said. "I'll take a wreath."

Liz Curtis Higgs

Liz Curtis Higgs is a native of eastern Pennsylvania. For ten years she hosted a popular radio program until she decided to make the move to professional speaking in 1987. She is the author of five books, including "One Size Fits All" and Other Fables, Only Angels Can Wing It, Reflecting His Image, and a best-selling children's book, The Pumpkin Patch Parable. She and her husband, Bill, and their two children, Matthew and Lillian, live on Laughing Heart Farm in Louisville, Kentucky. This story was originally published in Today's Christian Woman, November/December 1994.

CHAPTER 29

Reluctant Caroler

TERESA OLIVE

*O*h, come on, honey! It'll be fun," my husband, Jeff, pleaded. "Yeah, Mommy, please go caroling with us," my three young daughters chimed in.

I stared with gloom out the window at the pouring rain. It was a miserable night, even for western Washington. Then I looked at my family's expectant faces.

"Oh, all right," I growled. "Maybe we can sing 'I'm Dreaming of a *Dry* Christmas.'"

Jeff hugged me, undaunted by my lack of enthusiasm. I felt more like staying home with Scrooge than caroling in the rain with our Bible study group. Directing two Christmas musicals—

added to an endless round of shopping, programs, and parties—
had given me a bad case of "Bah! Humbug!"

By the time we met our group at a nearby trailer court, the
rain was mixed with sleet. I gritted my teeth as the wind whipped
the icy fragments into my face. No one else seemed to notice the
weather, though, as they all called out cheery greetings to us.

We sloshed up to a brightly lit trailer, singing "We Wish You
a Merry Christmas." The door opened a crack, but no one came
out on the covered deck.

Then, as we were leaving, a silver-haired lady peeked out.
"Thanks for the carols," she said. "My neighbor was robbed last
week, and I'm afraid to come out after dark."

The lady at the next trailer had no such apprehensions. She
braved the freezing rain to applaud enthusiastically after each
song. Afterward, she insisted we all come inside for cocoa and
cookies. She seemed oblivious to the gallons of water we dripped
on her floor. Her eyes were glued on the children as they gobbled
down cookies. Her face glowed with pride as she showed us
pictures of her own far-away grandkids.

By the time we left, I felt warmer in more ways than one.

We had started to pass by the next darkened trailer, when
someone in our group called out, "Wait! I think I see Christmas
lights inside." We began singing "Silent Night," softly, in case the
residents were asleep. The outside light came on, and an elderly
man stepped out on the covered porch to listen. I thought I saw
tears glistening on his cheeks.

After we ended, there was silence for a second. Then the man
said, "That was beautiful. I wish my wife could hear you. She

loves carols, but she . . ." His voice cracked, and he cleared his throat. "She's got cancer and can't come out."

We stood stunned for a moment. Then someone suggested, "Why don't we try singing up on the porch?"

The man smiled for the first time, a little-boy grin that lit up his face. "Oh, that would be great! I'll leave the door open and go listen with her."

Somehow we all managed to cram onto the tiny porch. We sang "O Holy Night" through the open front door. Luciano Pavarotti would have cringed at some of the sour notes, but we didn't care. We were singing for the audience behind the door, and for the audience above the rain clouds.

Several carols later, the man returned to the door with that little-boy grin still on his face. "She says to tell you thanks. It meant so much to her."

Impulsively I asked, "Would you mind if we came in for a minute?"

My husband and children stared at me, almost as surprised as I was by my new attitude.

But the man acted as if twenty unexpected guests was an everyday event. "Of course, come on in," he said, motioning us into the tiny trailer.

I half expected to see a room full of gloom and darkness. We found the exact opposite. Yes, the frail woman propped up on the living room couch was obviously very ill, but her dark eyes sparkled in her weathered face. Even the room seemed to reflect her joy. Christmas lights twinkled cheerfully on a tree, and the scent of cinnamon candles filled the room.

We asked a few questions and discovered they had four children scattered across the globe. "Unfortunately, none of them can make it home for Christmas this year," she said, "but maybe next year." I marveled at her ability to hope for joy next Christmas instead of dwelling on the pain of the present one.

Then she told us of her two-year battle with bone cancer, which had ravaged most of her body. She brushed aside our expressions of sympathy.

"I'm not afraid," she declared, "I know where I'm going. As soon as I leave this old body, I'll be with my Lord Jesus."

Then she sighed. "The hardest part is wondering which of us will go first."

Surprised, we looked at her husband.

"Congestive heart failure," he explained. "Doctors can't do anything for me." He took his wife's hand and smiled, "But that's okay. We don't want to be apart for long."

Before we left, several people promised to visit them and bring food on Christmas Day. Then we sang one last song: "Joy to the world! The Lord is come . . ." The miracle I saw in that room reminded me of the one in Bethlehem: riches in the midst of poverty, joy in the midst of tears.

I realized I had crammed so many things into my life during the last few weeks that I'd no longer had room for my Savior. How could I have shut Him out, even for a second? I opened my heart wide to welcome Him back, and felt His love and peace flood in.

Teresa Olive

Teresa Olive is a homemaker and free-lance writer. She lives a very simple life in the woods of Burley, Washington, with her husband, Jeff, and their four daughters. She has written five books and numerous articles. This article was originally published in Moody, December 1993.

CHAPTER 30

Dining with the Shepherds

VIRGINIA OTIS

*A*part from family gatherings on Christmas Eve, where we'd light candles depicting Jesus' entrance into this dark world and tell the Christmas story or joyfully pack treats in Christmas baskets for the needy at home and abroad, the time I ate dinner with a group of shepherds in Israel is my favorite Christmas memory. The idea originally came to my husband, George.

He wanted to have a Christmas feast with the Bedouin shepherds who lived around Bethlehem. It would be a wonderful time to share the story of Jesus with them, he thought, and tell how God had specially honored their ancestors on that spectacular and holy night. So, with the help of two dear friends, one Jewish and one Arab, the word went out to the desert that two crazy Americans were inviting shepherds to come into town for dinner.

When we arrived, they were already seated on well-worn cushions placed on the ground in the tent shelter we had prepared. Apparently *their* clock—the sun—was more accurate than ours.

Our friends made the formal introductions. The shepherds met our smiles with countenances marked by curiosity and caution. Their leathery grooved faces revealed the harsh reality of lives spent on the rugged slopes and valleys of Israel's rocky terrain.

I sat off to the side. Their society is very patriarchal; the only other female present was a Bedouin woman who was preparing roasted lamb over an open fire. But even though I was not in the middle of the group, I could feel the enormous power of this encounter.

The first order of business was to eat. We had a delicious meal of mutton and couscous covered with pine nuts. I couldn't help noticing the unusual utensils—their hands. Soon it was time for dessert, and we were each given steaming cups of pungent black coffee, fresh dates, and oranges. The shepherds began to relax, some settling down on their elbows to get ready for the story they had been promised.

George cleared his throat and began: "Centuries ago God sent an angelic choir to announce the birth of His Son to a group of shepherds in Bethlehem. Even though they did not possess great status in that society, they were God's first choice.

"You see, God loves shepherds. Long before this great birth, God chose a young shepherd boy, David, to become king over Israel. The God of creation saw something special about these 'keepers of the sheep.' Now they had been given the biggest news story of all time. They had the high privilege of being the first to announce this event to a spiritually hungry world."

As I listened to George speak, I was reminded of how God so often chooses the "foolish things of this world" to put the wise to shame. I wondered how these rough-hewn shepherds, many of them Moslems, were receiving the message of the Christmas story. My concerns were soon allayed. When George was finished, the shepherds smiled at us with toothless grins and offered their symbol of friendship, a common pipe. Later, George suggested we all get together again some time. All of the shepherds gave us enthusiastic nods of affirmation.

As we sat together in the afternoon shade, I reflected on the significance of this moment. Then, as though jolted by the Holy Spirit, I turned in the direction of the sheep grazing close by and was reminded of Jesus' words to His disciples: "Other sheep I have which are not of this fold; them also must I bring."

My gaze went from the sheep to the black-clad Bedouin woman who sat in the shadows, one of many born into a culture and religious system that offers little incentive or hope to women. How lonely she appeared. I went over to her and stooped down at her side. Even though I was smiling, my heart cried out, *Oh Lord, please bring Your light into this woman's darkness. Share Your tender mercies from on high. May Your Holy Spirit touch her life as He has touched my own.*

As I sat with this dear woman, the words of the song "Down from His Glory" came flooding into my heart and I began to silently worship: *Oh how I love Him, how I adore Him, my breath, my sunshine, my all in all; the great Creator became my Savior and all God's fullness dwelleth in Him.*

I pray that this story inspires all who read it to look beyond the sometimes lavish Christmas celebrations we all enjoy to include "the others" who have not yet safely entered the Good Shepherd's fold. We bring them in so that they, too, might worship the King this and every Christmas!

Virginia Otis

Virginia Otis is the territorial co-ordinator for LYDIA Prayer Fellowship in California, Hawaii, and the U.S. Pacific Islands. Her husband, George, is president of High Adventure Ministries. They have four children and ten grandchildren. Virginia has been praised for her gifted, inspiring, and challenging teaching, which often centers on the subject of how God can raise up Christian women as godly role models for others.

CHAPTER 31

Happy Birthday, Jesus!

SARA WHITE

*M*y father and mother taught me the value of traditions, especially at Christmastime. Proverbs 13:22 says, "A good man leaves an inheritance to his children's children," and I believe that word *inheritance* means more than just money and possessions. It means a legacy of values, traditions, truth, morality, character, and memories.

I want to leave a legacy to my children that they will pass on to their children—something that is stored up in their hearts. My parents gave me that kind of inheritance, and my husband, Reggie, and I are passing this same kind of inheritance on to our own children, Jeremy and Jecolia.

We home school our children. One reason is very practical:

Home schooling is the only way we can provide stability for our children's education since Reggie and I travel so much—and we usually take the kids with us. Another reason is that home schooling enables me to spend twenty-four hours a day with my kids, teaching them and molding them and passing on my faith and values to them. It's part of an overall process of leaving our kids that inheritance of memories, faith, and values. Another part of that process is the way we celebrate Christmas.

When our oldest, Jeremy, was very little, we began a tradition that we continue to this day: We have a birthday party for Jesus. We decorate the house and invite friends over. We put up balloons and a big "Happy Birthday" banner. Some years the kids and I bake a birthday cake, and some years I buy a cake from the bakery, since Christmas comes during football season, which is often very hectic. We light the candles, sing happy birthday to Jesus, and just have lots of fun.

Often we invite Reggie's teammates and their families to the party, but some years we just have our own immediate family. And, of course, people often drop in on Christmas day. They see the cake and party, and say, "Whose having a birthday?" And we say, "Jesus!" They laugh, surprised, and then join in the celebration.

A store in Milwaukee recently sent us a wooden candle stand with a carved plaque that reads, "Happy Birthday, Jesus," and we've made it part of our birthday party. At the bottom of the stand is a little pouch or gunnysack, which comes with cards that you fill out and place in the pouch. The cards read:

———

My gift to Jesus is

_____.

Each one of us writes down our gift to Jesus: "My gift to Jesus is to have a daily quiet time with Him this year," or "My gift to Jesus is to be kind to my brother or sister this year." These cards can be kept as reminders throughout the year. It's something we can all do—adults and children.

We still have the other traditions of Christmas—a Christmas tree and presents. When we give our gifts, we tell our children the story of the wise men who brought gifts to Jesus. "We're like those wise men in the Christmas story, bringing gifts to each other to celebrate the birth of the baby Jesus," we explain.

Reggie always reads the Christmas story, and of course, being a preacher, he's wonderful at animating the story, doing different voices for different characters and really bringing the story alive. No matter how young our children were or how excited to open their presents, Reggie always read the Christmas story first on Christmas morning.

Some Christian parents make Santa Claus a part of their Christmas, while others practically treat Santa as if he were something evil. In our family, Santa isn't an issue. We don't invite Santa Claus to our birthday party for Jesus, and we don't chase him off, either. It's hard to explain the concept of make-believe to tiny children, so we just ignored Santa Claus when they were preschoolers. I felt that if I said that Santa Claus, the Easter bunny, and the tooth fairy were real, they'd wonder if Jesus was make-believe when they found out the truth about these make-believe characters.

As our kids began seeing this man in the white beard and red suit at the mall or on TV, they'd say, "Who's that?"

We'd answer, "Oh, that's Santa. He's a make-believe character."

When they got older and asked more questions about Santa, we told them about a real man named St. Nicholas who was a friend to little children and gave gifts and money to the poor. We also explained that the world has taken the story of this wonderful man and changed it for commercial purposes, calling St. Nicholas by the name Santa Claus.

In our home, Christmas is not about fantasy. Christmas is about the ultimate reality: Jesus Christ.

Sara White

Sara White is the wife of Reggie White, the Green Bay Packer defensive lineman who is the NFL's all-time sacks leader. Sara and her husband formed Big Doggie Records to make an impact on the lives of kids through positive messages. During the NFL season, she is host of her own television show, "Sara on the Sideline." Aired on Green Bay's CBS affiliate station, she gives viewers a behind-the-scenes look at the Green Bay Packers in action.

CHAPTER 32

The Joy of Giving Your Faith Away

VONETTE BRIGHT

*T*he happiest season of the year for most people is Christmas. Certainly it is the most meaningful time for my family and me. My favorite collectibles are Christmas ornaments and decorations, which I have purchased or have received as gifts from all over the world.

Often Christians complain about the commercialism of Christmas as retailers focus their marketing efforts toward busy shoppers. I don't condone commercialism, but, since it's going to happen anyway, I do think we should take advantage of it.

For example, Hong Kong, Singapore, and Tokyo are wonderful at Christmas with colorful lights that produce spectacular scenes on the sides of buildings. There, where the message of Christ is not well known but where Christmas is an elaborate commercial event, believers have a great opportunity to share the true meaning of the season. In our country, we, too, can take advantage of the extravagant commercialism and share the joy of Christ's birth with others.

Even though we entertain hundreds of people throughout the year, I save our biggest social events for the month of December. Since people are more likely to think about Jesus and His coming during this month, it is a natural time to share our faith openly—with friends and strangers alike.

Henrietta Mears, the great Bible teacher and author, taught me to experience Christmas with *gusto*. My husband and I enjoyed several Christmases in her home before we combined our households and were together for nine years. She insisted the house be decorated soon after Thanksgiving, and she planned every available date we could manage for entertaining.

Our first Christmas together we drove into Los Angeles to purchase a Christmas tree. Miss Mears explained to us on the way how much she enjoyed the festivities surrounding Christmas. For her, if "a little" was good, "a whole lot" was even better. I soon learned that in a twenty-room house unless the decorations are colorful and massive they get "lost in space." Of course, with Miss Mears's warm, outgoing, and enthusiastic personality, nothing ever ended up lost.

Miss Mears wrapped presents for weeks before Christmas. At the same time, packages came for her from all over the world.

Eventually, gifts were piled so high around our huge tree that my dear husband would be horrified.

Bill has great compassion for the poor and he always felt that we may be lavishing more on ourselves than others. For this reason, my husband and I give gifts to an organization that reaches out to poor families rather than to each other. We generally only give token items to each other at Christmas.

We make sure, however, that our children, family, and close friends are well cared for. Just like Miss Mears, I enjoy lots of presents under the tree and save much of our gift giving for Christmas. Bill indulges my whim and allows me to celebrate Christ's birthday by giving presents to our many loved ones.

As I've said, though, our greatest joy at Christmas is "entertaining with a purpose." Among our favorite holiday events are the teas or brunches we hold where we invite people who have not accepted Christ as Lord. We ask a speaker to come and share on such topics as "The Real Meaning Behind Christmas Traditions" or "God, the Greatest Gift." During the message, the speaker will explain how an individual can ask Christ into his or her life and begin to trust Him as Savior. In closing, one of us will lead a prayer of faith.

We then hand out cards to our guests, asking them to jot a note if they would like to attend a Bible study or get together privately at another time for one-on-one fellowship. Their responses help us know how to follow up in their lives.

This type of hospitality is something everyone can practice. By entertaining with a purpose, Christmas will become more meaningful for your guests, and you will be privileged to give the greatest gift of all—our Lord Jesus Christ—to others. A friend and colleague, Barbara Ball, and I have seen so many benefits from social gatherings like this, that we recently published a book on the subject, *The Joy of Hospitality*.

Christmas can be in your hearts every day of the year when you share Christ with others, but there is just something extra special when you share His love during the season that we celebrate His birth. I pray for you a very merry next Christmas!

Vonette Bright

Vonette Bright is the wife of Dr. William R. Bright and is cofounder with him of Campus Crusade for Christ International. Born in Coweta, Oklahoma, she taught in the Los Angeles school system from 1949 to 1952; received honorary doctorate degrees from Los Angeles Bible College and Seminary in 1979 and from King Sejong University in Seoul, South Korea, in 1985; and was named a distinguished alumni by Texas Women's University in 1984. Vonette founded the Great Commission Prayer Crusade in 1972, was a member of the original International Lausanne Committee for World Evangelization, served as chairman of the Intercession Working Group from 1981 to 1990, organized the National Prayer Committee and served for nine years as the chairman of the National Day of Prayer.

CHAPTER 33

The Wonder of Advent

LISA ROBERTSON

*P*repare the way of the LORD." Both the prophet Isaiah and John the Baptist gave this commandment to herald the coming of the Messiah. I am reminded of these words as our family prepares for Christmas again this year. We have an annual tradition of staging a private Christmas play for friends and family, which is our personal way of announcing and celebrating the birth of the Christ child.

During the weeks of preparation, I often think of myself as the producer of an extravagant and elaborate Broadway production. I am responsible for the props, costumes, food, and the performances of the actors. All of the preparations take place over a period of weeks; the show opens and closes in just one day.

The celebration of the Advent season has become the foundation or "script" for our production and helps us focus on the more significant Christmas themes. Advent usually begins the first Sunday after Thanksgiving. Our Episcopal church holds a dinner where each family brings a pair of garden clippers, a bucket of greenery from their yard, and a potluck dish.

The church provides wreath rings (small plastic bowls, each with an oasis for the center of the wreath) for everyone, along with five candles: three purple, one pink, and one white. Tim and the children love putting our Advent wreath together. Juniper, boxwood, holly, ivy, pine, and magnolias have all been a part of our wreaths in past years. The greenery is wrapped around the ring, and the candles are placed in it.

The color of the three purple candles represents royalty, penitence, and the blush of dawn before the light of Christ entered the world. The pink candle represents the joy we find in the Rose of Sharon, our Lord Jesus. In the center of the wreath, the bowl is filled with greens, and the white candle, representing the purity of Christ, is placed in the middle. This candle will be lit on Christmas Day. Finally, purple ribbon is woven throughout the wreath and candles for a finishing touch of royal character.

These wreaths are a beautiful and fragrant addition to our home throughout the Advent season. During these four weeks we learn how God prepared the world for the coming of His Son. We talk about the ancestry of Jesus—Adam and Eve, Noah, Abraham, and David. We reaffirm that, while all have sinned,

God loved us so much that he sent His only Son to be a perfect and everlasting sacrifice.

Mary, Elizabeth, Joseph, and the angels come to life through the skits our children perform. One discovery we have made during our productions is that all the angels in the Bible began their proclamations with, "Do not be afraid . . ." Obviously, these are awe-inspiring heavenly beings!

Each Sunday one more candle is lit. First, a purple one accompanied by a passage from Scripture. Isaiah 2:1–5 is a favorite. The prophet Isaiah foresaw the coming of Jesus and wrote,

> Now it shall come to pass in the latter days
> That the mountain of the LORD's house
> Shall be established on the top of the mountains,
> And shall be exalted above the hills;
> And all nations shall flow to it.
> Many people shall come and say,
> "Come, and let us go up to the mountain of the LORD,
> To the house of the God of Jacob;
> He will teach us His ways,
> And we shall walk in His paths."
> (vv. 2–3)

The second Sunday we light another purple candle and think about John the Baptist, who called the people to repentance as they prepared for the coming of Christ. The third Sunday we light the pink candle and read Isaiah 35:1–10, which describes the glory of the Lord. Each week, the candles add more radiance.

Although the children take turns lighting each candle, their favorite is pink, since it represents the joyful news of Jesus' birth. On this Sunday we read Matthew 1:18–25, which features the Old Testament prophecy about the Messiah from Isaiah 7:14: "'Behold, the virgin shall be with child, and bear a Son, and they shall call His name Immanuel,' which is translated 'God with us.'"

Our Advent celebrations have helped us teach our children how and why to focus on Christ during a season that so many treat as a secular holiday. For me the Advent ceremonies stabilize my Christmas preparations. I still get frantic and overwhelmed as we approach Thanksgiving each year, knowing the pressures and hurried times that lie ahead. But because of what Advent has brought to our family, I feel confident that the Lord, in His sweet faithfulness, will carry us through another year and another "Broadway" production.

Lisa Robertson

Lisa Robertson was born and raised in Denver, Colorado. She graduated from Sweet Briar College in Virginia, majoring in Spanish. It was at Sweet Briar that Lisa met her husband, Tim Robertson, the son of Dr. and Mrs. Pat Robertson and now president of International Family Entertainment. Tim and Lisa are the parents of five children, ranging in age from six to fourteen. Lisa is active in her church, in an outreach ministry called Operation Smile, and with a Bible study for women she has led for the past twelve years.

PART FOUR

A DIARY OF

Christmas
Memories

FROM

YOUR HEART

TO THOSE

YOU LOVE

A Celebration Tree

TERRY MEEUWSEN

$\mathscr{A}$s I have put this book together, it's been a privilege for me to glimpse into the hearts and lives of these dear women who have shared their Christmas memories. I hope you have been touched by their moving stories as well, and have discovered many new ideas for your family to experience and enjoy this holiday season.

One afternoon, while working on the book, I had a wonderful telephone conversation with Lisa Robertson. A high-energy, creative mother of five, Lisa is full of imaginative ideas for holidays and special events that enhance each occasion with added significance and meaning. It happened to be the Easter season and she had just finished decorating an Easter tree.

"Lisa, tell me what you put on your tree," I said. "I have some darling Easter ornaments—bunnies, eggs, all the usual stuff—but I have never really found anything with much spiritual significance."

"Well, in addition to those things, I hang some traditional

ornaments as well," Lisa replied. "I wrap ribbon in and around the tree's branches, and this year I wrote down Scripture verses that were applicable to the season and tied them onto the branches."

Several days later I saw Lisa's Easter tree and was inspired to create one for my family, which would be filled with Scripture promises and Easter symbols that are meaningful to us. I continued to think about it over the next several weeks and began to envision a tree that could be decorated for *every* special occasion—one large enough to set on the floor and with enough height to hang ribbons and ornaments from its branches.

One afternoon I was driving my children home from school and had just dropped off a little boy who carpools with us. The next day was garbage pickup and people had set their trash cans and other disposable items at the end of their driveways. Suddenly, I slammed on my brakes.

"What happened!?" my children shouted simultaneously, lurching forward in their seats.

"*There it is!*" I exclaimed.

"What?"

"Where?"

Everyone peered out of the van in great anticipation.

"Our *celebration* tree!" I announced.

"You mean that dead thing next to those garbage cans?" asked Tory skeptically.

"It's perfect!" I was undaunted by their lack of enthusiasm. "Listen guys, I'm too embarrassed to put someone's dead tree in our van in broad daylight. Let's come back tonight. If it's still here, we'll claim it."

Later that evening we lifted that dead tree into the back of our van and hauled it home. Right now it's propped up against the back wall of our garage. But by the time you read this, it will be painted bronze, secured in a beautiful porcelain planter, and ready to be adorned with ribbons, ornaments, and Scripture verses relating to Christmas. We'll decorate it again for Easter and for other special holidays and events.

So many of the traditions we've adopted have been inspired by someone else. I hope this book will be an inspiration to you in establishing your own traditions. Be creative! The possibilities are endless!

We invite you to make this last section your very own. If you have special childhood Christmas memories, reminisce here. Is there a family recipe that is a holiday "must"? Jot it down. Whatever traditions you establish, old or new, record them on these pages. As you personalize this book, you will be creating a family treasure for your children and grandchildren.

If you're like me, it's sometimes easy to forget a special moment until an entry from a diary or journal brings the event rushing back as if it had just happened. I hope this exercise will inspire you to make the extra effort this year or next to plan for a Christmas that will be fondly remembered for many holiday seasons to come. Someday you'll look back and be glad you made the effort!

Merry Christmas!